HOPE WAS LOST, BUT GRACE WAS
FOUND

G. C. Carter

HOPE WAS LOST, BUT GRACE WAS FOUND
Copyright © 2020 by G. C. Carter

All rights reserved. No part of this publication may be reproduced, distributed, or transmitted in any form or by any means, including photocopying, recording, or other electronic or mechanical methods, without the prior written permission of the publisher or author, except in the case of brief quotations embodied in critical reviews and certain other noncommercial uses permitted by copyright law.

Although every precaution has been taken to verify the accuracy of the information contained herein, the author and publisher assume no responsibility for any errors or omissions. No liability is assumed for damages that may result from the use of information contained within.

Library of Congress Control Number: 2020924466
ISBN-13:   Paperback: 978-1-64749-304-2
           Epub: 978-1-64749-305-9

Printed in the United States of America

GoTo Publish

GoToPublish LLC
1-888-337-1724
www. Gotopublish. Com
info@gotopublish. Com

CONTENTS

ACKNOWLEDGMENTS 1
INTRODUCTION 3
REFERENCED SCRIPTURES (ESV) 37
EPILOGUE 39
SCRIPTURES 85

My dear reader;

I know the year of 2020 hasn't been the great year that many of us anticipated.

So many have lost so much due to coronavirus/covid19. Some have lost loved ones. Some have lost jobs and even homes.

In the midst of that, we've seen both civil and political unrest which sparked protests, riots and looting. This year has been filled with fears, anxieties, grief, anger, confusion.

***All scriptures in this book are from the English Standard Version (ESV) bible

This book is dedicated to all the broken and hurting people that may feel they have no reason to hope.

To the ones that feel unloved and unwanted, even by our Savior, Jesus Christ.

Be encouraged! He loves and wants you so much that He died for you! And you will never find any greater love than that!

ACKNOWLEDGMENTS

First and foremost, I acknowledge our Father God, and I give Him all the glory for any good that comes out of this book. It's His; I'm just the vessel He used to get it written. Thank You Lord for giving me the honor and privilege of being used by You.

I would like to acknowledge my family and friends that have inspired and encouraged me along the way and prayed for and with me. Especially my daughter, Montoya Jeter, who agreed to hold me accountable to write something every day. And my son-in-law, James Jeter, who has also been right there believing in me and encouraging me. I thank my son, Derris Smith, who in his own way has played a part in me being where I am now. And I must acknowledge my grandchildren, those near and far, who have encouraged me and definitely kept life interesting for me. I love you all, and I thank God for blessing me to have each one of you in my life.

There are so many others that have inspired and encouraged me along and have prayed with and for me and for this project.

I can't name everyone, but you know who you are. I love and appreciate each one of you and all you've done.

Last, but definitely not least, I must acknowledge my auntie, Brenda Draper who has been there for me all my life. Loving me, supporting me, encouraging me and teaching me, for being a true friend. I love you, my Auntie.

INTRODUCTION

In life, we all experience events so tragic that we feel there has been an "earthquake" in the very core of our being. And no matter how much we love God, we can still find ourselves so shaken, so dazed and confused, that elements of doubt, anger, grief, bitterness, resentment and unforgiveness can creep through the cracks left in our hearts. I know that because I've been there.

And if we're honest, we can lose hope and become angry with even God. We can easily begin to think He doesn't care about us. The stories in this book are meant to encourage and strengthen you. To assure you that no matter how bad things may appear to be, God is always there. He never leaves us. But so often, in the face of adversity, we can be guilty of turning away from Him. I hate to admit that I too, have been guilty of that.

Throughout my life, there have been times that I felt all alone, even with people all around me. Situations seemed so overwhelming that I thought I might die in the middle of them. As I got older, I began to learn how to put on the happy face, to wear that false bravado, while my heart was in pieces. I thought there was no way this God I had grown up hearing so much about loved me.

There was no way He cared about anything I was going through! I was just too bad and unlovable for Him to care! (I'd pretty much been told that anyway). I am so, so happy to tell you that both they and I were wrong. All I had to do was believe that He cared, and that He really did love and want me, just as I was! His Son Jesus had even died for ME!

As you read this book, please allow yourself to let our heavenly Father, His Holy Spirit, minister to you as only He can. He has done it for me, and He can do it for you! Right now, you may feel that all hope is gone, but God's grace and mercy is always available to those of us that choose to accept it. Allow yourself to embrace it as you read this book. God bless you.

THE THOUGHTS AND MEMORIES OF ELDARENE HARCUM

Well, gee! It looks like the more I do, the more I fall behind. Sometimes I feel like just giving up. These were Eldarene's thoughts as she went about her normal Saturday morning routine. Housework to finish, errands to run (lately it seems that list just gets longer too). And it definitely doesn't help that I'm staying so tired lately. Why? Is it because I have not been sleeping enough?

Well, no matter. Tired or not, I've got work to do. For some reason, as she began sweeping the kitchen floor, an old commercial began to play in her head. "I can bring home the bacon, fry it up in the pan." A wan smile crossed her face at that old memory. Well, I am bringing home the bacon, that's for sure. But I'm just too tired to fry it up in the pan.

Eldarene had indeed been feeling that something was wrong but for the life of her hadn't been able to identify exactly what it was. And it certainly hadn't dawned on her that five days ago, on Monday, April 18th was when the tiredness, the heaviness began to feel so burdensome.

April 18, 2009, two years ago had not been a good day for her. She was so glad she never had to relive that day, and didn't want to remember it either. Right then, all she knew was that she had been just fine until recently. She finished sweeping and prepared to mop the floor when suddenly her tiredness hit her like a ton of bricks.

Her legs began to feel like rubber so she stepped to the nearest chair and dropped onto it. Why am I so tired? As she asked herself that question, she realized that tiredness wasn't quite the right word. She was exhausted. Fatigued. Worn out. Kaput. Her get up and go had gotten up and gone. And it wasn't just her body, it was her mind as well. What in the world is going on? Maybe I should make an appointment with Dr. Easterly. I sure can't go on like this! Lord Jesus! Lord Jesus..........

At the mention of the Savior's name, not only did Eldarene feel exhausted; now an overwhelming sadness had seemed to envelop her and rise up in her all at the same time. She felt hot tears burn in the back of her eyes. What is wrong with me? What is this? And as the tears began flowing down her face, she thought "I am not a crybaby"! I'm stronger than that! What is going on? But as she asked that question yet again she realized that the answers she sought were already deep inside of her.

Buried in the memories of her past. Suddenly all those painful memories were rising to the surface. NO! I will not do this. For two years I've worked so hard to put all that behind me. To get over it and get on with my life. I want the past, those old hurts, to stay right where they belong.......IN THE PAST!

She thought of Jesus Christ, but would not allow herself to call His name again; hadn't really meant to the first time. Why should I call on Him? Where was He when I needed Him most? Where were the love, all the grace, and mercy I've heard about and believed in all my life? Hadn't I been faithful to Him? Hadn't I worked hard in the church singing in choirs, volunteering in different programs and even held different positions on the church board? I did all that because I really did believe He loved me and oh, how I loved Him. I thought He cared about me. But now I know that He doesn't love me.

How could He? There's no way a loving God, a loving Father, would abandon His child in her time of need. Two years ago, after all the countless prayers I prayed believing He would answer, but He didn't. I was pleading for Him to help me, but He only deserted me, and I've had to learn to make it without Him. And haven't I done well for myself? Yes indeed. You bet your bottom dollar I have, thank you very much.

At that thought, Eldarene lifted her head and straightened up in the chair. She didn't realize just how much she had cried until she saw the puddle of tears on her kitchen table. Puddle? It looked more like she'd cried enough to fill a small pond. She thought to herself, "never again". As she reached for paper towels to clean the mess, she glanced at the clock and realized it was now going on ten o'clock. Where did the time go? It was shortly after eight when she set about doing her housework. Did she waste all that time crying over what couldn't be changed?

Crying over spilled milk is what her Papa would have called it. Shame on you, Eldarene Harcum, she thought as she set about finishing her housework. She deliberately kept her focus on the tasks at hand and thought she was doing quite well. She hadn't realized that after her earlier crying episode she seemed to have a little of her pep back. Not much mind you, but enough to do what needed to be done.

It was shortly after noon, and Eldarene was now ready to face the world. To look at her composed and perfectly made-up face, no one would have ever guessed that only a few short hours ago she was in her kitchen crying a small pond on her kitchen table. Already she was focused on her to-do list, for she needed to keep her mind occupied. As she settled into her cream-colored 1999 Toyota Camry, she opened the console to find one of her soft rock CDs. She forgot she'd taken them out when she took the car to have it cleaned. She thought about going back in the house to get them, but decided the radio would do just fine. She found her favorite station and immediately heard Lionel Richie singing "Hello. Is it me you're looking for?" Any other time she would have hummed along, but for some reason she did not want to hear that today.

Hmmm! Why was that? She'd always really liked that song. She scanned to find another soft rock station, but for some reason all she could find was a gospel station. She thought that was unusual because any other time there were clear radio stations for any kind of music you wanted to hear.

Just then, Shekinah Glory's "Broken" began to play. Definitely not what she wanted to hear and yet she was powerless to change the station. She felt those pesky tears welling up again and fought with all her might not to cry. She would not cry again, and especially not in public. Besides, there was no time for tears now, as she'd just pulled into the parking lot of the Piquine Community Bank to complete the first errand on her list.

As the song ended, Eldarene turned off the radio and the car engine. She checked her makeup in the rearview mirror and deemed herself ready for the task at hand, on which she had already begun to focus.

At exactly 2:30 Eldarene exited the bank with a feeling of accomplishment. All was well with her accounts and her stocks. She definitely had no money worries, that's for sure. Yes, she felt the accomplishment, but oddly, no peace. She wondered why, but didn't think about it too long. She was happy to know she was okay financially. But money didn't own her, she owned it. Her Papa always taught her that. Now, on to the next stop.

Fingers n Toes Nail Salon for a little pampering. She was getting it all done today, manicure and pedicure. She thought she might go with cotton candy pink nail polish this time. That always made her feel feminine and pretty when she was feeling out of sorts. She was glad she'd had her hair done after work yesterday. Once her fingers and toes were done she knew she would feel like a new woman.

When she stepped out of Fingers n Toes at 5:08, Eldarene felt like she was walking on air. She felt beautiful. The memory of early that morning was now pushed far back into the recesses of her mind. She knew she was in control of her emotions again.

Now, on to pick up her dry cleaning, from there to the public library, and then on to the Piquine Food Market (her least favorite errand) to do some much needed grocery shopping. She knew that would take a while because she'd waited until she was low on pretty much everything. "Oh well! Let me go ahead and get this done" she sighed to herself as she got out of the car.

Eldarene slowly made her way through the market. Up and down each aisle to make sure she didn't forget anything she needed because she definitely didn't want to have to return too soon. All of a sudden, and she didn't know why, it struck her as strange that she hadn't seen any of her co-workers since she'd been out. Piquine was a small town and anytime you went out you were likely to see someone you knew. Not that she knew very many people yet. She'd gotten "sort of" close to a couple of co-workers at Lillenbragg's EAP, where she had been the office manager for the last eighteen months. As a matter of fact, one of them kept inviting her to go with her to church, as if Eldarene Harcum needed that. The rest were acquaintances, someone to say hello to when you saw them and to discuss work-related issues in the office.

She really hadn't had time to meet anyone else because her work days were usually so long. Even some Saturdays were spent at the office if she fell behind on paperwork during the week. Between her job, her housework and the errands she often needed to run she just didn't have time for a social life. And Eldarene liked it that way just fine. As long as she was busy, as long as her mind stayed busy, she didn't have to worry about remembering things she didn't want to remember. Yes, she liked her life just fine this way, and except for Papa, there was nothing she would change.

By the time Eldarene finished loading the groceries in the trunk of her car and was ready to head home, it was 8:43 p.m. "Not bad! Not bad at all", she thought, giving herself a mental pat on the back. Now, as her stomach growled, she wondered what she wanted for dinner. It had to be something light and quick because she hoped to curl up in bed with a good book no later than 11. She decided she didn't want to cook. She'd stop along the way and grab a nice healthy, tasty salad. Light, yet filling. And now, she'd like to enjoy a little soft rock during the drive home.

Eldarene had forgotten that the only reception she'd been able to get earlier was that gospel station so when she turned on the radio she heard the end of "Breathe on Me" by Eddie James. Oh no! Not that again! She scanned to find another station more to her liking. Right now it didn't even have to be soft rock. Anything would be better than listening to that gospel station! She scanned again, and once again, that gospel station was all she could find.

She thought, "This is just crazy". Any other day you could hear pretty much any genre of music you wanted. She thought about turning the radio off, but a silent ride home just didn't strike her fancy. She decided it was just music after all. She could deal with it for the five miles she had to go.

She heard Jekalyn Carr declaring God to be bigger than anything. Next, she heard J.J. Hairston singing that his (J.J.'s) hallelujah belongs to God. By the time Luther Barnes started singing about God's Grace, she'd decided she'd had enough; she just couldn't take it anymore and turned the radio off. God's grace? God's grace??? Where was God's grace when she needed it? Suddenly the exhaustion and that peculiar sadness enveloped her again.

As she pulled into her driveway and put the car in park the quiet was broken by Norman Hutchins singing "Jesus I Love You". That had been one of her favorite songs. She used to lead it when she sang with the Gospel Chorale. And…..Hey! Wait a minute. She'd turned the radio off. She knew she had. How in the world? But of course there was a logical explanation, just had to be. She'd accidentally hit the knob and turned that radio back on. That's all there was to it. Just clumsiness. Only in the back of her mind, she knew that wasn't the case.

That radio came on with no help from her whatsoever. But she didn't want to think about that right now. She was just too tired to try to figure it out. She just wanted to get everything in the house and put away and get ready for bed. By the time she'd finished, it was 10:43 p.m. Okay, she could still be in bed by 11, reading herself to sleep. She reckoned that overall, the day was quite an accomplished one.

By the time Eldarene brushed her teeth and freshened up it was 11:07. A little later than she'd planned, but she was almost ready for bed now so she reckoned it was still in good time. She changed into her favorite nightshirt, the one with the pandas. She couldn't explain it, but for some reason that nightshirt gave her comfort, kind of like Linus and his blanket, she guessed.

A sad smile played around her mouth as she thought of herself as a 47-year-old woman needing a "security blanket" or "security shirt" in this case. Just before slipping under the covers she looked at her cotton candy fingernails and matching toenails. Even though she still liked it, it seemed that the joy the cotton candy polish had brought her earlier had worn off. She didn't feel pretty anymore. Only tired and sad.

She sighed, slipped under the covers and reached for one of the books she kept by her bed. Actually, she didn't think she could handle a book right then. Maybe a magazine. The latest issue of People would do nicely.

She settled back onto her nice fluffy pillows and opened the magazine. Suddenly she yawned, one of those great yawns that stretch your mouth to the max. Before she knew it, the magazine slipped out of her hand and to the floor as she drifted off to sleep.

Suddenly, she was jarred awake by the sound of someone calling her name. It was 12:01 a.m. Not calling exactly. Someone "boomed" her name. This was the best and only way she could describe it. She jumped out of bed, heart racing, and shaking all over. She grabbed the Louisville slugger her Papa had given her when she was a little girl for she was sure someone had gotten into her house. And if so, whoever it was would find out she could still hit a home run.

As she crept out of her bedroom to search for whomever that booming voice belonged to, she struggled to remember if she had set her alarm. She was almost positive she had as her habit was to do so as soon as she came in. Her ears strained to see if she could hear the sound of movement in any other part of her house, but there was nothing but silence.

She made her way to the living room and checked the alarm. It was set just as she thought it would be. Then through the dining room and into the kitchen. Everything was as it should be. She then searched the rest of the house to further ease her mind. She then searched the rest of the house; bathroom, the guest bedroom and bath, the closet in there and the hall closet and found nothing.

As she went back into her bedroom to check her bathroom and closet she sure was glad that she didn't have a basement or an attic to check. Satisfied that all was well, she went back to bed.

She was back in bed, but couldn't go back to sleep for a while. She began to ponder the strange events of her day. Well, of what was now her "yesterday". It had begun with her crying as she had yesterday morning. Then there was that crazy thing with the radio. What was that all about? It was as if she'd been forced to listen to gospel music instead of the soft rock she liked. Then she remembered how the radio had turned itself back on last night.

She knew if she even tried to tell anyone else about it they would think she was out of her mind. And honestly, wasn't she beginning to wonder about that herself? What other explanation could there be?

She looked at the clock on her bedside table, 12:32 a.m. And that's another thing. Why on earth am I suddenly watching the clock so much? I don't exactly like to waste time, but neither have I ever been a clock watcher. What is happening to me?

Then she remembered that booming voice calling her name. Could it be that I am imagining all this? Am I losing my mind? Am I ready for a rubber room?

She pictured herself in a straight-jacket, sitting on the floor of a very small room that had rubber squares lining every inch of it. She didn't know if what she pictured was accurate and she really didn't want to find out if it was. Maybe I do need to see a psychiatrist though, as well as Dr. Easterly. She hoped he could recommend a good one. But for now, all I want to do is sleep. A nice, long and peaceful sleep.

As long as there was no need for her to be in the office, Sundays were the one day in a week she could allow herself to sleep until noon. And boy did she need it. It's the one day in a week that after a nice long sleep, she got up and dressed for the day, usually cooked a full meal, simmering in the crockpot while she washed windows or cleaned the oven or did any other chore she hadn't done on Saturday. Anything she could do to keep herself, and her mind busy.

Eldarene finally felt sleepy again and settled down under her nice warm covers. This was more like it. Nitey- nite world. And she was fast asleep.

ELDARENE HARCUM!!! That booming voice again! Eldarene sat straight up in her bed, but this time she didn't get up. She couldn't get up. It was as though she was paralyzed, but not with fear. At least not with the same fear she felt when she heard that voice boom her name earlier. No, something other than fear held her captive.

Strange, but this time the voice sounded vaguely familiar. Not comforting in any way, just familiar somehow. Without hesitation she called out "Who's there? Who are you? What do you want?" Even as she called out she found herself thinking once again that she must be losing her mind. There's no one here but me. She thought if she could get up and just walk through the house it would clear her mind.

She tried to get out of bed but found that she still couldn't move. She wondered if she'd had a stroke or something. She couldn't move to reach the phone and she'd lived alone for two years now so there was no one close by to help her. Was she going to die here alone? She didn't know, but oddly enough, she didn't think so.

She knew something was happening. Something she'd never experienced before. But what? Once again she wondered what was going on and if she was bound for a rubber room. She resigned herself to the fact that she was powerless to stop whatever was happening, so she might as well not even try. Ever what this was, it was certainly stronger than she.

Suddenly Eldarene was whisked from her comfortable bed and any remaining hope of sleep back through time to her wedding day. At least that's what it seemed like to her. It was as though she was actually, physically reliving the events of that day. She didn't like this one bit. NO! Why can't I stop this? I don't want to remember. She'd worked so, so hard to forget. To put it behind her and leave it there. Why is this happening to me? And why now?

It was Saturday, April 18, 2009. Eldarene was so happy she could hardly contain herself. Happy and nervous, for she was about to marry the man of her dreams, Minister Durwood Layton. Tall, handsome, intelligent Durwood.

He was 6'2", slightly heavy but not overly so. He was pleasingly plump she guessed you would say. And that hair. Naturally curly salt and pepper, cut close. A bit younger than she, he was 42. He had the most beautiful brown eyes she'd ever seen. Their's had been a whirlwind romance, dating only eight months before he'd asked her to marry him, and of course she had accepted.

At the age of forty-five Eldarene had all but given up hope of ever being married and having a family. Besides, she loved him and she just knew he loved her. She'd dated a few men when she was younger, but nothing serious. Nothing like this. But when she first saw Durwood Layton she knew in her heart she wanted to be his wife and have at least one child with him, God willing. And now, her dream was about to come true.

Eldarene and her Papa, Deacon Horace Harcum had arrived at the Right Word Baptist Church at 11:30 that morning. Neither of them wanted to risk anything going wrong to make them late for her big day. Both were happy and excited. Since Durwood had arrived in Maydonia, Virginia and started attending their church, her father had taken a liking to him.

When they began dating, it was with his blessings. And when they announced that they were engaged, she thought Papa was even happier than she was, if that was possible. The only thing that would have made it even better was if her mother could have been there. But her Mama had died when Eldarene was ten years old. She was killed by a drunk driver while coming home from girls night out with some of her friends. Since that time it had just been Eldarene and her Papa.

For some reason, her mother's family had never liked her father. They never thought he was good enough for their Pearlie Mae Beames. So once the funeral was over, the contact with them ended. They never even wanted her around them for holidays, which hurt Papa deeply because he wanted his baby girl to grow up as a part of her mother's family. But she was still Horace's daughter so they wanted nothing more to do with her.

In spite of that, she never felt unloved or unwanted. Her Papa had always wanted only the best he could give her. He did his very best to raise his "Ribbons" (he called her that because she loved hair ribbons so much!) right, making sure they were both in Sunday school and church (even on Wednesday nights) just as they did when Mama was alive. He made sure she ate nutritious meals, made good grades, had regular medical and dental check-ups and he attended every parent-teacher conference his work allowed him to. She thought that all these years maybe Mama had been looking down from heaven smiling in approval of Papa and hopefully of her as well.

Eldarene realized she'd better pay attention to the time. It would take a while to get her makeup just right and she didn't want to have to rush at it. Not that she really needed makeup. Pearlie Eldarene Harcum was still quite pretty even at the age of forty-five. She was 5'7" and slim. She kept her hair colored and coiffed in becoming styles, usually cut short. She had the light skin of her mother and the green eyes as well.

She sat down in front of the mirror in the church secretary's office (she was the secretary at the time), and busied herself with her makeup. Her Matron of Honor, Mrs. Lawson, and her bridesmaid, Lenora Wilkins would be arriving soon. She'd known them all her life since they'd always attended church together. They weren't quite friends, she didn't really have any friends, but they were still the only women she wanted by her side on this special day.

At 2:15 that day, Papa had knocked on the door to ask if Durwood had called her. He hadn't arrived at the church and no one could reach him on his cell phone. Eldarene, worried that something was wrong, took out her own cell phone and called him, but got no answer. Surely he was on his way to the church. He wouldn't miss their special day if everything was okay.

He loved her and wasn't he as excited as she on this special day of theirs? Besides, after the wedding, they were to tell Papa the secret they'd been keeping. Durwood had insisted she wait until after the wedding and they would tell Papa together, as it should be. He'd said that he wanted them to do what was right.

It was 2:30 and the wedding was supposed to be starting. Her Papa should be escorting her down the aisle to give her away. But that couldn't happen yet because no one knew where the groom was. Was he okay? Had there been an accident?

Eldarene was so worried that she begged her Papa to please go to Durwood's house to see if he may be there ill or something. She also hoped that maybe their paths might cross between the church and his house. But Horace Harcum wasn't about to leave his baby girl. He asked one of the other deacons to go over and see about the groom. Half an hour later the deacon returned and asked to speak to Horace alone.

As the memories kept resurfacing, Eldarene's tears had actually soaked the front of her nightshirt. So much for the security of the panda shirt. She wanted this to stop. But she couldn't stop it for she was still unable to even move. She couldn't get busy to free her mind. She thought maybe she'd fallen asleep and was dreaming about it for some reason. But this didn't feel like she was sleeping. This was something she really couldn't identify, and she didn't like it one bit. She'd be glad when it was over.

She was back to her wedding day. As Papa had talked to the deacon, she knew something was terribly wrong. She couldn't hear them for they had distanced themselves from the office door and they obviously were whispering. Or at the very least they were speaking with really low voices.

She wanted to know what was wrong. Durwood was her fiancé and she had a right to know.

Had he been terribly hurt in an accident? Could he be at the hospital wanting, needing her by his side? Or was he dead? She desperately wanted, needed to know and yet was so afraid to hear the answer, so she waited. Her Papa would tell her what was wrong.

A few minutes later Papa did return holding a piece of paper in his hand. The look on his face told her that all was definitely not well. Sensing that something was very wrong, Mrs. Lawson and Lenora Wilkins exchanged uneasy glances and eased out the door. Eldarene never even noticed them leaving.

Right then she could only see her Papa. "Papa? Papa, what's wrong? Tell me what's wrong? Has something happened to Durwood?" But all Papa could do was shake his head. He sat down in one of the deck chairs, the one opposite her. She could tell he was searching for the right words to say and the wait seemed like an eternity.

Finally, he told her that as far as anyone knew, Durwood Layton was fine. He didn't appear to be home as his car was gone and he didn't answer the door. But he had left a note taped to his front door. At the mention of the note Papa's eyes had filled with tears. She saw that his hand shook a little as he handed it to her. Her heart was racing, and her body quivered in fear of what the note might say.

She opened it and couldn't believe her eyes. She thought this must be someone's cruel idea of a joke. Her beloved Durwood would never betray her like this. He just wouldn't. She reread it and had to admit that it indeed appeared to be his handwriting.

In the note he'd written: "I know today was supposed to have been my wedding day. But I cannot marry Eldarene because she is pregnant with another man's child. As an ordained minister of God, I cannot marry a woman of such moral laxity. I will be away for a while to work through the pain this has caused me".

She felt as though someone had given her a punch in the belly and knocked all the air out of her. She was dizzy and confused and she was gasping for air. And the pain. The pain felt as though it was eating her alive. And Papa. Poor Papa. What must he be thinking and feeling? She couldn't bring herself to look at her father, so she looked over his head at the clock on the wall. It was 5:08 p.m. She didn't realize so much time had passed.

After her Papa left the office without saying a word, Eldarene, stunned and confused, changed out of the beautiful wedding dress she'd chosen and dressed in the jeans and t-shirt she had worn to the church. As she packed everything, she prayed, Lord, please, let this be a horrible nightmare. Please let me wake up and see that all is well. Please God! Please!! But even as she prayed, she knew this was very real. She wasn't dreaming this nightmare, she was living it. She tried to find her father so they could go home, but he was nowhere to be found.

When she pulled up in their driveway, she saw that her Papa's car was still there. He'd obviously gotten someone else to bring him home instead of coming back with her. Inside she called to him, but got no answer. She carried everything into her room then went to find him. She needed to talk to him to explain that yes, she was pregnant, but the baby was Durwood's.

She hadn't been with anyone else, and had only been with Durwood once, in a moment of weakness. Before he came along, she wasn't a virgin, she'd experimented in her younger days, but she hadn't been with anyone in so many years that she thought she might be pretty close to reclaiming virginity. Of course, she wouldn't tell Papa that last part. She knocked on his bedroom door and called to him, but got no answer. She didn't know if he was in there, but still called to him. "Papa, please let me explain." After a couple of minutes and still no response she began searching for him throughout the house.

She finally found him in the basement at his workbench, just sitting there staring off into space. "Papa, may I talk to you? Please Papa, I need to explain something to you. Please?" Finally, he turned to her with sad, wet eyes. Say what you need to say Eldarene. "Eldarene?" How that hurt because for years she'd been his "Ribbons", but she thought it best to leave that alone right now. She began to tell him the truth about the whole situation. Yes, she was eight weeks pregnant, but Durwood was the only man that had been in her life for years now. She hadn't dated since her late twenties, and that was the truth.

As embarrassing as it was, she even told him how in a moment of weakness she and Durwood had made love. She assured her Papa that as much as she loved Durwood, she repented for that and vowed she would never let that happen again until they were married. And she had been true to her vow, no matter how much Durwood had wheedled and cajoled she stuck to her vows. He'd tell her it was okay because they were getting married anyway, God would surely forgive them. But she still didn't give in.

At some point, as she told her dear Papa the truth, he moved over to sit beside his daughter and was now holding her hand. She knew he believed her, but needed to hear him say he did. "Papa, please believe me. No matter how bad a thing is, I love and respect you too much to lie to you." Her Papa had assured her that he believed her. He knew his baby girl very well and knew she wasn't one to try to lie about anything she'd done.

She'd always been one to face the music, a characteristic of hers he'd always been particularly proud of. He hugged her and told her he reckoned they both needed to turn in. It had been a long and tiring day. As she started up the stairs Papa called to her. "Ribbons, you're my baby girl and I'll always love you. Never forget that." "I know Papa. I love you too." She was so glad to hear him call her "Ribbons" again.

Once upstairs Eldarene washed her face and brushed her teeth. She was so numb and drained that she didn't even bother to change her clothes. She just stretched out on top of the covers in her jeans and t-shirt. She was trying not to think about all that had happened over the course of the day. Right then, she didn't think her mind could handle it. She finally heard Papa come up from the basement, but something about his footsteps didn't sound quite right.

All her life she had heard her father walk through the house and knew the comforting sound as he walked on the Congoleum floors. Papa took a few more steps and then she heard a crash in the living room and knew that the television had been knocked over.

She jumped up and ran to see what had happened and found him on the floor clutching his chest and writhing in pain and struggling to breathe. She grabbed the phone and dialed 911. As she knelt by her Papa the dispatcher asked how long he had been on the floor in pain. She'd looked at the clock and saw that it was 8:43. She reckoned it had been about a minute, if that.

Once the doctors and nurses had Papa situated in CCU, they let her go back to see him. She'd never seen her Papa looking so frail, like only a shell of the hale and hearty man she'd always known. He was always so full of life, love and laughter. Maybe he'd had a cold now and then, but that was it as far as she knew. Her papa was a tall man, 6 ft. 1", and as long as she could remember had always weighed around 200 lbs. But right now he seemed smaller and almost foreign to her.

The nurse explained that he'd had been sedated, so he didn't even know she was there. She thought the pain of the day's events had knocked her for a loop, but seeing her father like this and the thought of losing him was more than she could bear. She began to pray to God begging Him not to take her Papa from her.

"I know this is my fault Lord, so please don't let my Papa suffer anymore because of my sin. God I'm so, so sorry. Please raise my Papa up out of this. I know you can. You raised Lazarus from the dead, so I know you can heal my Papa." The nurse came back in and told her it might be best if she went home and tried to get some rest. They would call her if anything changed. But she wasn't going anywhere and told the nurse she would be in the waiting room.

Once in the waiting room, Eldarene saw she was alone. Good. She was in no mood for small talk and possibly answering questions about her father's condition. She knew her dear, sweet, loving Papa needed a lot of prayers, and went right back to silently talking to God the Father. Again begging Him, the Healer to have mercy on her Papa. As she sat praying she realized there was an emotional stew boiling inside of her; all the emotions of earlier that day along with the guilt and fear she felt over Papa's heart attack.

She didn't realize she'd spoken aloud when she said "GOD I NEED YOU. MY DADDY NEEDS YOU. PLEASE GOD HELP US. FOR THE SAKE OF YOUR SON JESUS, HELP US!" Then she broke down and cried hard and loudly. Her sobs shaking her whole body as she cried. Once she had regained some composure she went to the bathroom to wash her face and thought maybe a cup of coffee would help. She realized she'd had no food or drink except for a small glass of apple juice since early that morning.

In the bed Eldarene shifted a little and seeing she could finally move she tried to get up. It was a no go. She desperately wanted to stop the memories but it was as if she was still a held captive by them. Usually she could just focus her mind on a particular task and get busy to stop the memories from coming forth. She could squash them at will. Usually. But not this time. She realized her panda shirt, her "security shirt" was pretty soaked, but couldn't get up to change it. She'd never known one person could cry so much

Her mind went right back to the night of Papa's heart attack. She came out of the bathroom and was digging in her purse to take out change for coffee. When she looked up, she saw a doctor and a nurse approaching her. She couldn't remember the doctor's name but knew he was the one treating her Papa.

She felt as though a huge rock had been dropped into her belly. She so much wanted it to be good news, but deep down inside she knew it wasn't. "Ms. Eldarene Harcum?" The doctor asked. "Yes, I'm Eldarene. My Papa???" The doctor and nurse wanted her to sit down. They wanted to know if she was there alone. Was there anyone she could call. No, no one.

"Ms. Harcum, We're very sorry but your father has expired. He transitioned peacefully at 11:07. We can call the funeral home of your choice if you'd like. Is there anything we can get for you? Some water or some coffee maybe?" "No. Nothing, thank you."

Eldarene was on autopilot. As the nurse gave her Papa's personal belongings, she couldn't help but think about how drastically her world had changed in less than twenty-four hours. She'd awakened to what she thought would be her beautiful wedding day. By now she should be Mrs. Durwood Layton and should be on her honeymoon headed to Jamaica. Instead of joy and wedded bliss she'd suffered abandonment and betrayal and now the loss of her Papa, the only person in the whole world that she knew loved her.

Even at the age of forty- five she felt like an orphan. She was all alone now, at least until her baby was born. She'd make sure that he or she always felt loved, wanted and protected. But as fate would have it, that was not meant to be. She suddenly felt a pain in her abdomen, then another and felt wetness spreading through the crotch of her jeans. Another pain so excruciating that she cried out, getting a nurse's attention. Before she knew it she was on a gurney being swiftly carried to the women's Center.

She heard words like hemorrhaging and miscarriage. She tried to pray. All she could say was "No God! No!! Please no!!!" She lost her baby at 12:32 a.m. The doctor told her one of the nurses heard her scream at 12:01 and went into action, but there was just nothing they could do. They figured the loss of her father was too much for her in her condition. (They had no earthly idea that this was the culmination of one long nightmare of a day). So that was it. Her punishment for the sin she had committed. Now she was left to suffer the consequences with not even a hint of love to ease the pain.

Her God had shown her no mercy. No mercy, no grace, no love. None at all! She felt a type of coldness settling in her heart, then throughout the rest of her. She thought, "If that's how it is, so be it. I have no one but myself now. No more praying to a God that's not even listening to me. No more church. No more singing in choirs. No more. Never again!"

Eldarene was awakened around 7a.m. that morning when a nurse came to take her vitals and to tell her the doctor would be in shortly. All she knew was that she needed to get out of there. Papa had made all his choices for his memorial service and burial long ago, but she still had to choose a time for the memorial service. There was no family to notify because like her, her father had been an only child and his own parents had been deceased for years.

She thought she needed to call the pastor, as he would give the eulogy. And there were pallbearers to choose. Deacons from the church she guessed. When the doctor came in she told him of all she had to do. He was reluctant to let her go home, but since she didn't have anyone to help her, he discharged her. But it was on the condition that she would take it as easy as she possibly could and would see her own doctor in a week. If anything happened before then, she had to come back to the emergency room. She promised she would.

The memorial service was the following Tuesday. People spoke to her, shook her hand and hugged her, but she hardly knew what they were saying. Words of comfort she supposed. She was only functioning on autopilot, not even trying to hear or feel anything. She was afraid if she did the pain would kill her or at the very least, drive her insane.

Once the memorial service was behind her, she began the task of going through the strongbox Papa had told her contained all of his important papers and sorting through all his other belongings. She had never been through anything like this, but she reckoned she'd figure it out as she went. "My Papa." If she could have her Papa back, she knew everything would be okay. But she knew she would never have him back, only memories of him. But at least they were mostly good ones. Up until……she got busy so she could stop that thought in its tracks.

As she sat in her bed, she couldn't stop the memories and it seemed she couldn't stop the tears either. She could feel how much her eyes had swollen. She needed a cold washcloth to put over them. She also needed the bathroom in the worst way. She wiggled a bit to see if she could move now and was so glad she could get up. Maybe while she was in the bathroom she would get at least a brief reprieve from the painful memories of the past. She didn't realize she'd already cried her way through the worst of them.

As the memories played on she went about freshening herself up and putting on a fresh nightshirt. She carried a cold cloth back to bed to put over her eyes. Good thing it was Sunday and she didn't have to go anywhere because it would take some time for the swelling to go down. As she got back in bed she noticed that her covers were a little damp. They would be okay though. She'd just throw them back for a while so they could dry. Her nightshirt had caught most of her tears. She lay back in her bed, hoping she didn't have to remember any more of that hurtful part of her life. All she wanted was some nice, peaceful, dreamless sleep. She finally got what she longed for.

That Sunday Eldarene awoke shortly after 1 p.m. Her eyes were still swollen from all the crying, but for some reason she felt more peaceful than she'd felt in a long time. As she showered and dressed, she kept thinking about how strange yesterday had been. She had never wanted to remember her wedding day again. She couldn't help but remember her Papa and the night he died though, because she missed him so much every day. And her precious baby. She tried not to think about how it would have felt to hold that little boy or girl in her arms to love and care for with all her heart. For two years she'd done everything in her power to avoid remembering these things. But last night the memories came forth like an erupting volcano, the hot lava pouring its way out of her heart and mind. She hoped she would never have to experience anything like that again.

Showered and dressed, Eldarene went into the kitchen and busied herself putting a container of her frozen beef stew in the crockpot. She thought she would probably make cornbread later. Right now, she thought she might do her windows. She went into her living room, prepared to start with the windows in there when suddenly she felt like all she wanted to do was…. Nothing.

She wanted to relax on the sofa and maybe watch a movie. She looked at the sofa and was so tempted to put everything away and stretch out on it. She somehow knew she no longer had to keep herself and her mind busy to avoid painful memories. On the tail of that she thought, "yeah, but what if I'm wrong? What if I think I can relax and then those memories creep up again? Better safe than sorry." So she started washing windows.

That evening, after her supper of beef stew and cornbread, (now that was yummylicious), Eldarene cleaned the kitchen and began to prepare herself for work the next day. Mondays at the office were usually long and hectic, so she wanted to get a good night's rest.

She laid out her clothes and shoes, and made sure her work bag was in the chair near the front door so she could grab it on her way out. With all that done, she thought she would read for a while, then get herself a good night's sleep. She'd been wanting to read "The Notebook" for a while now and decided tonight was a good time to start it.

After reading for about an hour, Eldarene was so sleepy she could barely see the words. She put the book on her bedside table and turned off the lamp and bid the world good night. It wasn't long before she was dreaming, something she didn't do very often. As if programmed to do so, her dream picked up where the memories of the past had left off the night before.

In the dream, she saw herself going about the streets of Maydonia, doing all she needed to do after Papa's death. As she did so, she saw many people she had known, most of them were from the church. She couldn't ignore so many fake smiles and words of sympathy, all the hateful, accusing stares, and the whispers that weren't really whispers at all. Even in the dream she felt the hurt, the embarrassment, and the loneliness. In the dream, it was now six months after her Papa's death. Painfully, she was selling the house. She'd tried so hard to continue living in the only home she had ever known, but it proved to be too much for her. She had to get out of that house, out of that town.

Now she was dreaming of her move to Piquine, Virginia, 75 miles from Maydonia, and the start of a new life. She saw herself stepping into her new home. After that, there was no more dreaming, only a deep, sweet sleep.

At 7:30 Monday morning, Eldarene woke up feeling more refreshed than she'd felt in a long time. She made her bed, as was her habit. She then showered, applied her makeup and dressed for the day.

After having a slice of toast and a small glass of orange juice, she grabbed her workbag, set her home alarm and headed out into the bright morning sunshine. She thought she didn't remember seeing the sun shine so radiantly before and didn't even realize she was smiling quite radiantly as well. In fact, she smiled so much that day that some of her coworkers complimented her on the beauty of it. She felt pretty again and this time it had nothing to do with cotton candy pink nail polish! And so it went that whole week, no matter what problem arose.

Shortly after nine that following Friday night, Eldarene had finally finished her paperwork for the day and was ready to get home and do absolutely no work. She surprised herself with that thought, as she was usually busy until she was ready for sleep. Wow. What a change. She wasn't sure, but she thought it might have something to do with her strange Saturday - into-Sunday morning event. Whatever it was she had to admit she liked what she was feeling.

She wondered if this was what the beginning of emotional healing actually felt like. If that was so, she wasn't naïve enough to believe she'd arrived, not yet anyway. But at least she thought she was on the right path, intentionally or not. She also wondered if there would be any more days and tears like she experienced over the weekend. She certainly hoped not.

Once in bed, she found she couldn't sleep just yet. She didn't really want to read but she didn't want to lie there looking at the ceiling either. She thought about finding a movie on TV, but decided she didn't want that either. That's when old habits tried to kick in. Her mind was busy thinking of a chore to do until she got sleepy.

Bathrooms always need cleaning she thought, and was about to get up to do just that when she heard a small, still voice say, "Be still Eldarene. I want to talk to you". It sounded like that same booming voice she heard Saturday night, only this time it was soft and gentle. Still she became a little apprehensive, wondering if she was about to be locked into and paralyzed by her memories again. "No. Please, No. I can't go through that again. I just can't." She started to the bathroom to busy herself, but hearing that voice clearly speak to her stopped her.

"Be still my child." That voice again. "Who are you? What do you want? She asked." The owner of that voice replied. "You used to know My voice Eldarene. You used to know Me. There was a time when we talked often. A time when you believed in Me with all your heart. You never doubted My love for you. But when Durwood Layton came into your life, that all changed. I gave you signs to let you know that he was not the right man, that I didn't send him to you. I even gave you a dream in which he turned into a snake and bit you, but still you wanted him. You had to have Durwood Layton."

"You even dismissed the dream saying it was caused by something you ate or something you saw on television. You no longer had a full and pure heart for Me. You began to seek Me less and less. Things you once would have talked to Me about, you began to talk to him about instead. You sought his counsel instead of Mine. You talked to Me only briefly and even then only when it was convenient. Yet you spent every free moment of the time I gave you talking with him. He became your god Eldarene. You gave him My glory."

"And you know that I am a jealous God. I'm the One that sacrificed My own Son for you and yet you worshipped him. But in all this I have never stopped loving you and neither did I leave you as you thought I had. I've always been right here, still watching over you. It was you that turned away from Me. I wanted so much to protect you, but you wouldn't let me."

"So my child, as much as it hurt, I had to let you suffer the consequences of your actions before you lost your life, your very soul. Durwood would have killed you. But before your death, he would have abused and tortured you in every way. I had to make you see the truth about him."

"As for your Papa, it was time for him to come home. He already knew that and was prepared. His one regret was that he didn't get to walk his little 'Ribbons' down the aisle to give you to your husband. He didn't want to leave his baby girl all alone. But he still trusted me enough to ask that My will be done, and not his. He trusted Me to take care of you. And your baby never belonged to you. He was always mine and I brought him home as well."

"You asked Me to help you in all of these, but you asked amiss. You said some of the right words, but in your heart you didn't trust Me enough to ask that My will be done instead of yours. You didn't believe in or trust My plans for you."

"More and more, you wanted it your way. Eldarene, I want you to come back to me. Let me heal and prosper you in mind, body and soul. Let me deliver you from the hurt, the pain, the unforgiveness of yourself and Durwood. Let me give you beauty for all the ashes as only I can. It's up to you my child. I love you and I'm right here waiting".

Eldarene hadn't realized that once again she was crying or that she was on her knees. She now knew what all the tiredness and sadness was about. All this time she had been carrying a heavy load that could have been lifted, had she not trusted herself more than God the Father. That peculiar sadness was repentance for her sins.

She thought she should have known this already. She began to pray a sincere prayer from the depths of her heart, "Oh God, I'm so sorry for my sins. Please forgive me for the sin of pride, for the sin of worshipping idols, for surrendering to the lust of the eye and lust of the flesh. Father forgive me for doubting you, and for turning away from You. For wanting my own will and way instead of Yours. Please forgive my disobedience. And please forgive me for any sins I've committed that I can't think of right now. Please deliver and cleanse this prodigal daughter, and take me back. In the mighty name of Your Son, Jesus Christ, I beg You to take me back. I never want to live without you ever again." And she meant it with every fiber of her being.

The following Sunday Eldarene couldn't wait to get to the church that her coworker, Daphne, had been inviting her to. The "This Side of Heaven" Baptist Church. As a matter of fact, hers was the first car in the parking lot. She prayed, "Lord, I don't know where You want to plant me, but I'm willing to do my part to find out. Please order my steps and let Your will be done. In Jesus name, Amen". As she entered the church for the first time ever, she had a feeling of coming home. She loved the atmosphere there so much that she continued attending and in one month she knew this indeed was home. And as for the gospel music she once shied away from, it was all she wanted to hear now. She was even singing in the choir.

Six months later, as she was downtown leisurely window shopping, Eldarene heard a familiar voice call her name. She stiffened a little as she turned and saw that it was none other than Durwood Layton. She was taken aback because she hardly recognized him. She'd thought if she ever saw him again her heart would be full of anger and dislike, if not outright hatred. But what she felt was pity. He'd lost a lot of weight and was now in a wheelchair. They exchanged pleasantries, as polite people do and she said goodbye.

As she turned to walk away, he called her name. "Yes Durwood?" He began to tell her how sorry he was for the way he had treated her, and that he hoped one day she could and would forgive him. He then proceeded to tell her that as he tried to run away from her and their wedding that day he was barely fifty miles away when a drunk driver ran a red light and hit him head-on. He'd almost died. He said he knew what she was thinking, that he deserved it. But Eldarene assured him that she didn't think that at all.

"Durwood" she said, "By the grace of God I have received His forgiveness, and I have learned to forgive myself and you as well. Honestly, I feel sorry for you and I sincerely wish you well." And she meant it. As she walked away, she thanked God for the change in her. She knew she wasn't where she needed or wanted to be, but she could honestly thank her Heavenly Father that she wasn't where she used to be.

She was finally free of the past. She knew she would still make mistakes, but thank God she knew she was free from the bondage of sin. The chains of unforgiveness, of pride, of fear and of idolatry had been broken. She knew she would always be in the process of becoming better for God's glory and that was just fine with her. She smiled a radiant smile and started to sing, "Freedom, freedom, freedom, freedom. No more shackles, no more chains. No more bondage, I am free". Yes, she was free. Free to live and enjoy life again. But more importantly, she was free to love her God again with all her mind, body and soul. And she liked that just fine too.

REFERENCED SCRIPTURES (ESV)

John3:16 (Jesus speaking): For God so loved the world, that He gave His only begotten Son, that whoever believes in Him should not perish but have eternal life.

Exodus 34:14: For you shall worship no other god, for the Lord, whose name is Jealous, is a jealous God.

Deut. 31:6b: For it is the Lord your God who goes with you. He will not leave you or forsake you.

James 4:3: You ask and do not receive, because you ask wrongly, to spend it on your passions.

Matt. 6:10: Your Kingdom come, Your will be done, on earth as it is in heaven.

Jeremiah 29:11: For I know the plans I have for you, declares the Lord, plans for welfare and not for evil, to give you a future and a hope.

3John 2: Beloved I pray that all may go well with you and that you may be in good health, as it goes well with your soul.

Isaiah 61:3: To grant those who mourn in Zion---to give them a beautiful headdress instead of ashes, the oil of gladness instead of mourning, the garment of praise instead of a faint spirit;

Thank you so much for reading this book! It has been an honor and a privilege to be used in the writing of it. My prayer is that God may use it to help you in some way to bring deliverance and healing where ever and however you need it. God bless you!

EPILOGUE

Saturday, May 25, 2013 was an exceptionally beautiful day. There were no clouds in the sky and Mr. Sun seemed to be shining down his brightest rays especially for Eldarene. The birds seemed to be singing songs to serenade no one but her. The grass was the greenest, lushest she ever remembered seeing.

Aloud, she said, "God, I thank you for this special and beautiful day". It was her wedding day and this time she knew in her heart that all would be well. She knew that because from the moment Jason Garrett Noland had asked her for the first date, she had been asking God for guidance and had continued to do so every step of the way. This was especially important because Jason had a ten–year-old daughter that she loved dearly and never wanted to hurt for anything in the world.

As a matter of fact, his daughter, Jasmina had stolen Eldarene's heart when they first met. The child's mother had died over two years before, a victim of cancer. Jasmina was still having a problem adjusting to her mother's death because they had been so close.

Academically, she did well in school. She just kept herself isolated and would only converse if someone spoke to her first. And even then she responded mostly in monosyllables. Jason said she was a good child; he was making an appointment because he was just so worried about her emotional and social well being.

The following day, when Jason brought Jasmina to her appointment, Eldarene somewhat saw what Jason meant. Eldarene's own mother had died when she was ten, so she thought she understood a little of what the child was going through. She spoke to the child and sure enough, a "hello" was all she got, but it was enough for now.

Each week, when Jason brought his daughter to her appointment, Eldarene made a point of speaking to Jasmina, letting her know she was an important person too. With each visit, she and Jason became quite chatty with one another, even joking and teasing each other. Then when, one day he told her he had been visiting churches since moving to Piquine but hadn't found a church home, she invited him to visit her church, This side of Heaven Baptist Church. The following Sunday she was glad to see that he and Jasmina were there.

When service was over and Eldarene came down from the choir stand, she made her way through the crowd to speak to her guests. Jason asked if she would join them for dinner but she declined afraid of a conflict of interest. She knew she wasn't Jasmina's counselor, she was the office manager, but she didn't want to jeopardize the child's care or her own job. But when Jasmina looked up at her with those big, sad brown eyes and asked her to please come with them, her heart melted and she couldn't say no.

The three of them enjoyed a Chinese dinner and even Jasmina was talking and laughing. Not a lot, but Jason said it was more than he'd seen since her mother died. It filled Eldarene's heart with joy to be a part of it, and to hear the little girl's laughter. When dinner was over, as they each headed to their own cars, both Eldarene and Jason were surprised when Jasmina suddenly ran over to her and hugged her tightly. Neither of the adults knew what to say or do for a moment. Then she hugged the child right back with a tight, loving, and motherly hug.

For the last month of Jasmina's sessions, Eldarene explained to Jason she thought it was best that they did not date until the child was through. But she always made sure to let Jasmina know that she was so special to her.

Once the sessions were done, Eldarene, Jason and Jasmina spent more and more time together. They'd go on picnics, to dinner, to the movies or just enjoy ice cream and long rides. The more they were together the more she and Jason got to know each other, sharing things that neither of them had ever shared with anyone else. And she loved the fact that he was always a gentleman. A Christian gentleman. He had begun to end each date with a prayer, which she was really happy with. Even though she could see the man he was, she never stopped praying and seeking God's guidance.

Then, on Christmas eve, he and Jasmina came over to have dinner with her and to watch "Elf", the little girl's favorite Christmas movie. Eldarene noticed that Jason and Jasmina would often exchange glances and the child would giggle, but she didn't ask questions. Let father and daughter have their fun. They had no way of knowing that she already knew what their secret was.

At noon on Christmas Day, father and daughter arrived at Eldarene's, presents in hand, to share with her the dinner she had worked hard to prepare for them. After exchanging gifts, she started to get up to put dinner on the table, but Jasmina gently pushed her back down and giggled. "Not yet," she said. Then she looked up at her father and said "now Daddy". They both got down on one knee in front of Eldarene and as Jason presented a gorgeous diamond ring, they asked Eldarene in unison, "Will you marry us?" This time when she said yes, she knew it was in God's will. They didn't know that God's Holy Spirit had already told her this would happen and that

God sent her the family she'd always wanted. Since she and Jason were both approaching fifty, it was just fine if they never had a child together. She already had the gift of a child to love in sweet Jasmina. And every day she would thank God for her and she would cherish and care for her with all of her heart. And definitely Jasmina's father as well.

So now, today, May 25, 2013, was her wedding day. She was now Mrs. Jason Garrett Noland and new mother to Jasmina DeRiah Noland! And they were on their way to Hawaii for their honeymoon, all three of them. They'd made special arrangements so Jasmina could be a part of it too.

Mrs. Pearlie Eldarene Harcum Noland was truly glad she'd let God have His way this time. She knew that no matter what would come, she and Jason would stand together, hand in hand, standing on the firm foundation of Jesus Christ, the solid Rock. And she liked that just fine.

A HEART FOR MOSES

"Hi Miss Rita," shouted little Jakey Monroe. 5-year-old Jakey and his family lived two houses down from Rita Marie Lesslee. "Hi Jakey. How's my little man today?" She wasn't asking to make small talk. She really was interested in the children on the block. She knew that children were just as special as adults, maybe even more so. And she always wanted, in some small way, to make a difference in their young lives. (That was why she had become a teacher). And sometimes she even preferred a conversation with a child. They were a lot more honest and unpretentious. They had imagination. They could dream. These were things a lot of people lost along the road to and in adulthood. And it just thrilled her to see the world through their eyes.

As Jakey sped off on his little bike, Rita, still smiling, returned to her yard work. She had only to ask and one of the teenage boys in the neighborhood would gladly have done it for her, but there were times when she just wanted to do the yard for herself. The good Lord had blessed her with good health and she didn't want to waste that precious gift by waiting for someone else to do everything for her. And besides, it was a good exercise anyway.

As she worked she hummed an old hymn, "Revive Us Again", and thought about all the years she had worked with children as a second-grade teacher. How she loved her babies. Each year the children in her class meant even more to her as it became apparent she would never have any children of her own. She'd been a spinster, as her auntie called her, until her mid 50's when she'd met and married John Henry Lesslee. Their love was never filled with fireworks, but it was a solid, comfortable, fulfilling love. They understood one another very well. They prayed together, studied the Bible together, laughed together, cooked together and even cried together at times. Yes, it was a wonderful marriage for the seven years they had been together. But it was over now.

Fourteen months ago, John had been diagnosed with hypertension. They had changed their eating habits and had learned to spend more time relaxing to reduce stress. But his job as the project manager of a construction site was stressful. All the rain and some flooding had caused his crew to fall behind on a particular job and the client was giving the powers that be at Davis and Healy Construction a hard time, and those same powers that be, in turn, gave John a hard time. It proved to be too much, especially with him working in all the extreme heat that followed all the rain. Her John Henry had a stroke while on the job and for the five days he'd been in ICU, he never regained consciousness. How she missed him.

She was back to living alone, but she wasn't all alone though. She had two really wonderful and loving stepchildren. She was so blessed in that. She and Ricky Lee Lesslee, who lived in Dallas, Texas with his wife and two children usually spoke at least once a week. He was always asking if she was okay and if she needed anything. She would assure him she was fine and then he would catch her up on what was going on with him and his family. He always ended the call by saying "you be blessed Miss Rita". He had a really strong aversion to saying "goodbye".

Then there was Jackie Sue Lesslee, an unmarried photojournalist that traveled all the time, mostly in other countries. More often than not, she was the one that would call Rita as often as she could and would always ask if Rita needed anything. It was so hard for any of them to call Jackie with her travels and busy schedule. You could call her office and leave messages, but unless it was an emergency, it still would likely be days before she called back, if then. She was just that busy! Yes, Rita was truly blessed to have them in her life. She often thought how they could have forgotten about her once their father died. But they loved and respected her too much for that, a fact that she thanked God for daily! Her only regret was that she didn't get to be with the grandchildren as much as she would have liked.

"Hey Miss Rita. Why didn't you call me to do your yard work? You know I'm always glad to help you." It was 17-year old Jaimel Leonard. He'd been one of her second-grade students and boy was he a handful. Not a "bad" boy, just the class clown type. Mischievous. But he always made good grades and now he'd graduated high school with honors and was on his way to college on an academic scholarship. She was so proud of him. She always loved to hear him say that she was one of his greatest influences, and always thanked her Lord for that. How she loved being used to make a difference in children's lives.

"Hello Jaimel! How are you? There was no need to bother you." She laughed. "I'm not so old that I can't do a little yard work. Not yet anyway." They both laughed. She asked if he was ready for college and he said he guessed he was as ready as he would ever be. She assured him that he would be just fine. And she knew he really would. They chatted for a while, then he said he'd better get going to his part-time job delivering pizzas. She wished him a good evening.

After Jaimel left, Rita decided she'd done enough yard work for one day. It was time to get inside, take a shower and decide what would be for dinner. When John was alive, she enjoyed cooking and sitting down to dinner and sharing stories about their day, but now that she was alone, meals were a necessity and nothing more. And now that she was retired she was lonely, and that made meals even less enjoyable.

After a dinner of a baked potato and a salad, Rita did the dishes and decided she would watch "Wheel of Fortune", then "Jeopardy" and maybe there would be a good movie on the Hallmark channel. She just couldn't stand movies with all that nudity and profanity. Hallmark always had good wholesome movies. She settled down in her favorite chair and put her feet up on the matching ottoman.

She looked over at John's recliner and thought about how they would watch their shows together when his work allowed him to be home to do so. She felt that loneliness that was now all too familiar to her. "How I miss that man" she said to the empty room, with tears in her eyes. The "Wheel" was starting so she turned her attention to that. One of the contestants was an elementary school teacher. She hoped he would win. He didn't, but he did come in second and she thought, "Well, at least he wasn't at the bottom of the totem pole." Time then for Jeopardy. She liked to test her intellect with this show and she also learned a lot as well.

Halfway through Jeopardy, her phone rang. It was Mr. Elwood Dalton, the principal of Rocklynder Elementary School. A third-grade teacher would be out on maternity leave the beginning of the new school year. He knew Rita had recently retired, but would she be interested in substituting for six weeks or so of the new school year. Rita thought this was such a perfect opportunity. She was getting tired of the loneliness of her retirement. She thanked the principal and assured him she would be glad to fill in, God willing. Mr. Dalton said it was he that should thank her. They wished each other a good night and said goodbye. Rita was elated that someone would need her, at least for a while anyway. She thanked God and asked Him to please, let her be a blessing to at least one child, as she had prayed every day of her teaching career. "I just want to make a difference for you, Lord."

Finally, August 22nd and the beginning of the new school year had arrived. Rita was beside herself with joy to be going back to work even if it was temporary. As she made her way to the classroom, she saw some of the students she'd taught in previous years. A few of them even hugged her. When she got to her classroom, she put away her purse and lunch bag, wrote her name on the board, and looked at the roll book and the lesson plans, which was standard third-grade academics. The students began filing in and it felt like old times. She thought, "Okay Lord. Your will, Your way, as long as I make a difference."

When the students were all seated, she noticed a boy that was bigger and looked a little older than all the other children. She thought she remembered seeing him from time to time, but had never had the opportunity to speak to him. His name was Moses Dinforth. He wasn't dressed quite as well as the other children, and his clothes were a little dirty. There was an air of false bravado about him that instinctively told her this was a troubled child. She could see the mistrust in his eyes, and couldn't help wondering what his story was. She was careful not to single him out for anything that day. She was no psychiatrist or psychologist, but Rita had worked with children long enough to know that she needed to gain his trust. And she was determined to do just that.

After school ended that first day, Rita met in the lounge and chatted with the other teachers. After the general conversation, she asked the other teachers about Moses. One of them, Mrs. Shuler had him in her class the previous year, and according to her he was a "bad egg". She didn't know that labeling Moses had rubbed Rita the wrong way. Moses came to Rocklynd to live with his grandmother when he was a toddler. His grandmother was not only elderly, but was ill as well. She didn't know what the exact illness was.

As Rita heard this, it felt like a big hand had somehow reached into her chest and clutched her heart. Mrs. Shuler was still talking……."but that's no excuse. He just won't cooperate. I mean, so he stutters, and yeah, some of the kids make fun of him. But he needs to just buck up and learn to deal with it if he wants to make it in this world. He got to the point that he wouldn't even try to answer a question when I called on him, and that's just plain rude. Rita, I know you love kids. But take my word for it, that one isn't worth the effort."

Now Rita seldom got angry with anyone, but right now, hearing Mrs. Shuler speak this way about a child made her blood boil. It was teachers like this that gave all teachers a bad reputation. And she thought, "So many of us do it because we love those kids and want to make a difference in their lives. We sure don't do it for the money". Rita said she really needed to get home, there was something she needed to do. That something was to get as far away from this Shuler woman as quickly as she could. Rita just didn't trust herself to be in her presence right now, because she was on the verge of telling this woman a thing or two.

On the way home, Rita thought about Moses and prayed, "Lord, use me to make a difference. Let Your love flow through me and reach out to this child. You used someone to do it for me, so if it be Your will, You can use me the same way with him. In Jesus name, Amen." When she got home, she went in, put her bags down, knelt down and cried and prayed for Moses.

After a while Rita got up and went to wash her face. She didn't really want any dinner, but knew she had to eat something. She decided that a bowl of cereal would do. As she ate, she studied the lesson plan for the next day while wondering what she could do to make Moses feel like a valued student…..a valued person. Her mind went back to her own childhood, especially after the death of her mother, and how Mrs. Elsie Brentner had made such a difference in her life. She remembered how that precious lady had cared for her when no one else had. Well, no one except her grandparents, that is. How that dear lady made Rita Marie Hartner feel so loved. Helped her to believe in herself. But more important than all that, Mrs. Brentner had introduced her to a man named Jesus, and Rita's life had never been the same.

Rita Marie Hartner had been born March 23, 1955 to Will and Lacee Hartner. Her parents had eloped as soon as they were both eighteen, and shortly before their high school graduation. Three months later, they were expecting Rita. They had both intended to go to the college but they knew that plan had been changed. The plan had been that he would help Lacee first, then when she graduated secretarial school and had a good, steady job, she would help him through community college as he studied auto mechanics. But with a baby on the way, they saw no way to see their plans come to fruition. They knew that neither of their parents could help, and probably wouldn't want to. Both sets of parents were civil to them, but it was still made crystal clear that they did not approve of their marriage.

Will had taken a full time job washing dishes at Holly's Diner making seventy-five cents an hour, and Lacee was cleaning houses and doing laundry for two dollars a day. Not a lot of money, even in those days, but they had to make it work, especially with a baby on the way.

When Rita was born, her bed was a large wicker laundry basket until she outgrew it. Then she had to sleep between her parents until they had finally saved enough money to buy her a used crib. Lacee had been taught how to quilt and sew from the time she was a little girl and was able to make a thick quilt that served as a mattress for the crib. She also made little pillow and covers for her little girl as well as cute little dresses from scraps of the material she was able to obtain here and there. According to Lacee, life hadn't been the greatest, but it was as good as they could make it. And they were happy and so proud of their baby girl.

And her mother said things stayed pretty good for the first two years of Rita's life. There were struggles along the way, but they always had a roof over their heads and food on the table. And once in a while there was a little money to buy Rita a store-bought dress, or a toy. That was, until Will had disappeared shortly after Rita's second birthday. With no explanation or even a good bye, he just never came home from work one day. A worried Lacee, knowing this was uncharacteristic of him had asked his parents and everyone they knew if they'd seen him, but no one had. Or at least they said they hadn't. Lacee always suspected that Will's parents knew exactly where he was but didn't want her to know. She had even gone to the sheriff, but got no help there either.

Life after that became even harder for Lacee, but she was determined to take care of her baby girl the best she could.

Seeing how hard Lacee worked to provide for her baby, carrying Rita with her from one job to another, Lacee's parents asked her to come back home and live with them. She really didn't want to because the relationship between Lacee and her parents was still strained. But she knew she had to think about her baby girl and do what was best for her. So on Rita's third birthday, they moved in with her maternal grandparents.

Life had become better for Lacee and Rita. Grandpa Joe had managed to get Lacee a job in the factory where he worked, making much more money than she'd made cleaning houses and doing laundry. And since Nana Ruth was always home, she kept Rita with her while Lacee worked. Life was definitely better. Rita had been showered with all the love and affection her mother and grandparents could give her. She had more clothes, more toys, and definitely more food, especially more fruit, and that she really loved. Life was good until a month before Rita's tenth birthday.

Some time before Christmas the previous year Lacee had caught a really bad cold. She tried every home remedy they could think of and she even went to the doctor. The coughing would get a little better, then get worse again. Through all that Lacee was determined to miss as little work as possible, saying, "I got to take care of my baby girl".

Then one day in early February, she was feverish and too weak to get out of bed. Grandpa Joe had called Doc Davis who told them that Lacee had double pneumonia, and it was pretty serious. She really needed to be in a hospital, but she refused to go, and he couldn't force her to. He gave her a shot and left a prescription for antibiotics and cough medicine.

Rita, feeling helpless, thought that there should be something she could do to help her Mama, but didn't know what it could be. She had heard of people going to church, but no one in their house ever went, so she had no way to know anything about praying to God, asking Him to heal her mama. All she knew was that her Mama needed help.

A week before Rita's tenth birthday they buried her dear Mama. Rita couldn't even begin to explain how she felt inside. She hurt so bad all the time. She didn't know how to tell anyone that it hurt so badly. But it was as if her name was "Pain", as though it was her sole identity. And this wasn't something she could bandage up until it healed.

Even though she was still living with her grandparents, she felt like she was all alone. She had no idea where her father was or if he was even alive. She didn't even know what he looked like because he left when she was so young and she had never even seen a picture of him. She'd never met her paternal grandparents, so she had no help there. Even at ten, she knew the image she saw in the mirror wasn't any help because all she ever saw was a smaller image of her mother. And everyone else always said she was her mother's twin, apparently seeing nothing of her that resembled father.

Rita's Nana Ruth and Grandpa Joe did the best they could to help her, but they really couldn't because they didn't understand her and what was happening with her. They were simple, hardworking people that knew nothing about child psychology or anything of that nature. And they definitely knew nothing about Jesus Christ the Savior or His Holy Spirit, the Comforter.

They had both heard of Him, but had never had an interest in getting to know Him. So, as time went on, Rita withdrew more and more into herself and her grandparents pretty much gave up on trying to help her. Not because they didn't love her, but because they just didn't know what to do. They weren't mean or abusive to her in any way. They tried to hug her and love her as they had before, but the child would just stiffen up, not returning any affection.

She was fed and clothed and went to school like all the other children. They even went out of their way to buy her extra toys and such to let her know she was loved. But no matter what they did or said, she just didn't want to talk to anyone, didn't want to be close to anyone. They didn't know that she was afraid that anyone she loved or was close to would die and leave her as her mother had. And added to that, after her mother died she started stuttering when she talked. This made her a prime target for bullies, so she reasoned that her life was easier if she just didn't try to talk to anyone. Looking back, she could thank God that none of the bullies ever got violent with her. She was glad of that, but their verbal and emotional abuse had left wounds that seemed to take forever to heal.

Some of her classmates would make up cruel songs about her not having a mother or father. Some would call her "Stutter Nut", claiming she stuttered because she was crazy. Then there would come recess when none of the kids wanted to play with her. A few girls from time to time seemed to want to be her friend, but when the other kids made fun of them, they would drop her as if she carried a plague. She felt so alone now, and no one understood her. There was no way she could ever make them understand. By the time she turned twelve years old, she had begun to wonder why she was alive. She never thought of suicide or anything like that, but she just didn't see any point in being alive until one day a substitute teacher named Mrs. Elsie Brentner came along.

Rita was in the sixth-grade, short and a little plump like her mother was. Her skin was a light brown and her hair was long, thick, and coarse, also like her mother's. It was usually done in two braids with ribbons on the ends. Because of the way the other children treated her, she thought she must be really ugly. She wondered how she could look so much like her mother and be so ugly.

Her Mama was beautiful, and her brown eyes really sparkled when she laughed, which made her even more beautiful. This was what Rita was thinking during recess as she sat alone and stabbed at the ground with a stick. Suddenly, Mrs. Brentner was sitting beside her. "My, my. Why is such a pretty little girl like you sitting alone digging the ground what for?" Rita tried to answer, but all that came out was "I-I-I" so she gave up and dropped her head. She wondered why a teacher would want to sit with her and talk to her. And a pretty teacher at that.

She thought the teacher was almost as pretty as her mama had been, with her smooth black skin, pretty white teeth and brown eyes that seemed to shine like stars. She wore her salt and pepper hair in a bun on top of her head that made her look regal somehow. Mrs. Brentner asked, "Honey, are you always this quiet?", still Rita couldn't answer.

"Well, I expect when you have something you really want to say, you'll talk. But right now, it's about time for us to go back inside." She blew the whistle so the kids would line up. There were no more one-on-one moments between Rita and Mrs. Brentner that day. But it turned out that Mrs. Brentner was with them for two weeks and every day of that time she found ways to make the children feel special, feel loved. She had a way of letting them all know that they could learn and they could be whatever they wanted to be. A doctor, a lawyer, even an astronaut if they wanted it badly enough.

She was really great at inspiring children. And whenever she could, she found an extra moment and way to let Rita know that she was beautiful and she had to believe in herself. Mrs. Brentner just seemed to know somehow that Rita needed that encouragement even more than the other children. Rita had no way to know this, but the Holy Spirit had let the teacher know that this was a hurting and troubled child and that she, Elsie Brentner had been sent here especially for her.

By the last day of her assignment as their substitute teacher, Rita had grown to trust and even love Mrs. Brentner, and would talk to her a little when no one else was around. She couldn't understand it or explain it, but the teacher seemed to understand her and to really care about her. When Mrs. Brentner found a moment to speak with Rita privately, she asked the child if it was okay for her to come to their house and meet her grandparents. Rita's eyes lit up at the thought of the teacher visiting them. Mrs. Brentner explained that she would really like to be able to take Rita out with her sometimes, and that she had one special place in mind that she wanted to take her for sure. Rita, filled with excitement and anticipation, wondered where in the world a teacher like Mrs. Brentner would want to take her.

At 2 p.m. on the following Saturday, Mrs. Brentner arrived at the home of Rita and her grandparents. Nana Ruth greeted her at the door and welcomed her inside. Then she was introduced to Grandpa Joe. Rita, with no inkling herself as to what she was about to do, hugged the teacher tightly which surprised everyone there, even Rita. Her grandparents exchanged puzzled glances and knew there was something special about this woman.

The adults talked for a while, then Rita was called back into the living room. She had gone into her own room because back then children didn't stay in the room when adults were talking. Nana Ruth told her that Mrs. Brentner would be picking her up from time to time and taking her to different places, starting tomorrow. That would be Rita's first time attending church. Until she went to sleep that night, Rita wondered what it would be like. What did people wear to church? She didn't know if the girls wore hats like the ladies, or not. Would she need to wear one? She decided that whatever she had to wear, she would as long as she could be with Mrs. Brentner!

That Sunday morning, Rita was on pins and needles. She got up, bathed and dressed even before her grandparents got up. She had on what she thought was one of her prettiest dresses, had shined her shoes and made sure her hair was combed. So as not to make a mess, she only had a bowl of cereal and washed her bowl and spoon after she ate. After that, she couldn't be still while she waited for what seemed like an eternity for Mrs. Brentner to arrive.

Finally, Rita was walking into the Living Word Holiness Church, hand in hand with Mrs. Elsie Brentner. She'd never seen the inside of a church before and thought this was the most beautiful place she'd ever seen. The hardwood floors were so shiny, and the runner down the aisle was the prettiest, most vibrant red she'd ever seen. And those stained glass windows. She had thought they were beautiful from the outside, but seeing them from the inside made her feel like she was in the presence of royalty. Later, she would find out just how right she was.

When the choir marched into the choir stand, Rita saw that they were kids, some of them she knew from school. And those robes. They were so beautiful. Purple with gold trim. She thought she would give just about anything to wear one of those robes. But, she thought, I can't sing though. When they started to sing the first song, "O I want to see Him, look upon His face", Rita wondered who this "Him" was.

She thought if He lived in a place this grand, she wanted to look upon His face too. There were a couple more songs, then offering. Rita almost panicked because she had no money. But Mrs. Brentner, always knowing what to do, slipped a piece of fifty cent into her hand without anyone seeing. When it came their time to carry up their offering, Rita was proud to be in the number.

After offering came another song, then the pastor, Rev. Darryl Longwood, got up to preach. His topic was "What a Beauty You Are". Wow. Mrs. Brentner was always telling Rita that she was beautiful. And now, here was this stranger, this preacher, saying she was beautiful. She knew he wasn't talking just to her, but it sure felt like it. Could it really be true? Rev. Longwood read from a book something called the Scripture (was that like a prescription for medicine?) she wondered.

Mrs. Brentner opened her Bible and held it so Rita could see it. Psalm 139, verse 14. Rita read it too. "I will praise thee; for I am fearfully and wonderfully made: marvelous are thy works; and that my soul knoweth right well." After church, Rita tried to remember the whole sermon, but could only remember that Scripture. Mrs. Brentner told her that God willing, she would give Rita something to help her remember, if she wanted to come back, that was. If she wanted to come back?

Of course she wanted to come back. She'd loved it. And that Sunday, May 11, 1969, was the very beginning of her walk with the Lord. And the surprise the following Sunday? It was her very own Bible, a notepad and pencils so she could always take notes. Mrs. Brentner said that was very important. Two Sundays later, on May 25, 1969, Rita became a baptized member of Living Word Holiness Church.

Nana Ruth and Grandpa Joe weren't really happy about it, but they had given their permission if that was what the child wanted. They just wanted their granddaughter to be happy. She was a little hurt that they wouldn't be in attendance at her baptism, but she knew Mrs. Brentner would be there with her and she was glad of that. Giving her life to the Lord, accepting Jesus Christ as her Lord and Savior, was a decision Rita never regretted making. God had been so good to her, in spite of the hardships and struggles she'd experienced, she knew her God was always with her, taking care of her.

As Rita thought back over these things, her mind went back to Moses Dinforth. "Lord, how can I help him? You said to not let our good work be evil spoken of. In this day and time, if I manage to show special interest in this child I may be accused of some immoral behavior. She heard a soft voice speak to her faintly and say, "Trust Me to deal with that". "As You say Lord. You know what You're doing. Have Your way."

Then, one day, God unexpectedly gave her the opportunity she had prayed for in regard to Moses. Rita was shopping at the Sav-a-Lot when she saw Moses and his grandmother enter the store. His grandmother walked with a stoop and it seemed it took everything she had just to keep moving. The woman snapped at Moses to get her one of the riding carts, and he did so without a word. When he came back with it, Rita smiled at him, but he dropped his head, afraid to speak she guessed. Rita introduced herself to his grandmother, Mrs. Lena Dinforth, who made it clear she was not in the mood to hear of any trouble Rita wanted to say Moses was getting into at school. Rita assured her that he wasn't causing any trouble, in fact, he was the quietest, most well-mannered student she had.

At that, Moses, remembering how his last teacher talked about him, looked at Rita in disbelief, and then his eyes seemed to say "thank you". Rita then asked if Mrs. Dinforth and Moses had a way home. "We got feet, and that's good enough. The boy can carry most of the bags." Rita assured her that she would be happy to wait for them and drive them home. "What for? I ain't got no gas money to give you." Rita assured her she didn't want any money. She just wanted to be a help if she could.

As they pulled into the driveway she got a good look at their house. The exterior of the house needed a paint job, but you could see that Moses and his grandmother did the best they could to keep up the house and yard. Rita smiled and said, "Well Moses, let's, you and I, get these groceries in so your grandmother won't have to carry anything".

When they were inside Rita admired the neatness of the place, which made her wonder why Moses sometimes came to school in dirty clothes. Mrs. Dinforth thanked her, invited Rita to call her Lena, and asked if she would like to sit down, which Rita did.

Once you got past the grandmother's gruff exterior, she was quite a nice woman. She even began to share funny stories of Moses when he was younger. After about an hour of warm and friendly conversation, Rita told Lena Dinforth that as much as she was enjoying herself, she really had to go.

Lena, seeing that Rita was down to earth and not a saditty such-a-much, invited her to come back any time. And she did just that. She would always call first, and was welcomed every time. She didn't want to wear out her welcome, but she thoroughly enjoyed her time with them.

Then, one Saturday, when she felt the time was right, she invited Moses and his grandmother to please come with her to the church. The Dinforths exchanged glances and Moses dropped his head. Rita wondered if she had overstepped any boundaries. Had that prompting been her own instead of the Holy Spirit's? There was such an uncomfortable silence for a few minutes that Rita thought it would be best if she just apologized to them and left. When she stood up, Lena Dinforth asked her to please sit back down. As she did, she saw that there were tears in the grandmother's eyes.

Lena began to speak in a low and trembling voice. "I know you're a good and kind woman Rita. And I know you meant no harm. But I just don't think I will ever set foot in another church. She explained that for years she had been an active member at one of the local churches, she refused to say which one. She told Rita that as long as she had a good job, nice home and car, wore the right clothes and most of all paid healthy tithes and offerings, everything was good. And her being an upstanding member of the community didn't hurt either. Her pastor and fellow church members treated her with the utmost respect.

She was always one of the first people they would come to asking her to either chair a certain program or otherwise participate in various activities. She had been the church board president, vice president, and secretary. She sang in the choir. She prepared communion. She worked in the kitchen. Anything they asked of her, she was glad to do. Rita's heart sank at what she thought she was about to hear.

Lena continued. "Then, things began to change. My son had gotten a girl pregnant and the young woman wanted to have an abortion." But Lena's son would have no part of it and told the girl if she would just have the baby, he would find a way to raise it himself. So, when Moses was born, his mother disappeared and no one had heard from her again. Thomas, Moses' father, had gotten a job in another state and when they talked, had always assured her that he and his son were fine.

He'd found a very nice daycare for the boy while he worked. Then, he started dating another woman. Was even talking about marrying her. The problem was, he didn't know that she was already married until the night the woman's husband confronted Thomas in the parking lot of the movie house they'd just come out of. Thomas had tried to explain that he didn't know she was married and that he was sorry, but the husband was having no part of that.

Witnesses told police that her son, Thomas, had tried to walk away but the husband shot him in the back three times and her son had died instantly. Thank God Thomas had left three-year-old Moses to spend the night with a neighbor so he could play with her three-year-old son.

Needless to say Lena had gotten custody of her grandson. And that's when things at the church began to change. She was actually asked to "resign" her positions and her membership at the church because the whole situation gave the church a "bad name".

To be in any way associated with such "carryings-on" would cause membership and monies to drop and they just couldn't have that. They said they might be able to "play it down", but she was bringing that illegitimate baby in there every time she came as though she was proud of the whole mess.

As they were saying all this, she couldn't help thinking that if her husband Donald were still alive, there was no way he would take this calmly. He was a peaceful, kind and loving man, but when it came to his family, he could go off the deep end pretty quickly. But he wasn't there; he had been dead for over ten years by that time. She was alone. The things she was hearing some of her fellow church members say were so hurtful and unexpected that she kept pinching herself to make sure all that was really happening.

When everyone had finished having their say, Lena Dinforth had calmly responded by telling them they didn't have to worry. She and her grandson would never darken that door again, and they hadn't. Of course, that hadn't been all she'd wanted to say. And it sure hadn't been all she'd wanted to do. She'd really wanted to slap the tar out of them all.

But she was determined to not show them just how hurt and angry she was at them and later at God as well. She had never before felt so hurt, betrayed and abandoned.

But she had to think of her grandson. Moses had heard all they had said, whether he understood it or not. She was all he had, and she didn't want to set a bad example, no matter how young he was. If she let herself stoop to their level she would likely end up in jail, then where would her grandson end up? No, she had to think of him above everything. She and Moses never entered not only that church again, but none of the others in the area either.

As Rita listened to Lena, she sensed that it was a story that had never been told to anyone else. It was obvious she had carried that hurt and betrayal for some years. Rita was blessed in that she could honestly say she had never suffered any real hurt from any of her church family, but she had often heard it said that "church hurt" was the worst kind of hurt. And now, listening to Lena's story she could believe that to be true. She couldn't help wondering what church Lena was talking about and was glad her church family wasn't like that.

Sure, there were a few saditties there, and a few disagreements in every church, but overall her's was an accepting and loving church family. Lena and Moses were both crying and poor Moses hugged and held his grandmother, doing his best to console her. By now Rita was crying with them and moved over to hug them both. She silently prayed for them as she did so.

As soon as Rita got home that evening she knelt by her favorite chair and cried and prayed. Not just for Moses this time, but for his grandmother as well.

As she prayed she said "Lord, I don't understand how people that say they love You could hurt someone like that. How is that bearing the fruit of Your Holy Spirit? How is that showing Your love to hurting people? I know there is no way that the past can be changed."

"But Lord, would You please use me in such a way that Lena and Moses would feel Your love flowing through me? Tell me what to say and what to do to make a difference."

"Dear Lord, Lena needs You, but that child needs You even more. Oh God, for the sake of him, I ask in Jesus' name that You please save this child and his grandmother. Amen."

That night Rita couldn't sleep. The faces of Lena and Moses stayed before her pretty much all night. Her heart was so heavy for them, for their very souls. She wanted so much to make a difference in their lives. But she knew she was only a vessel, an instrument to be used.

God was the only one that could really make the difference they needed. Of course, the change would happen when Lena decided that she wanted and needed that change. Rita desperately hoped and prayed that Lena would somehow make that decision soon, especially for the love and life of Moses. She instinctively knew that if Lena turned back to God, Moses would follow.

Rita was determined to show Lena Dinforth that not all "church folk" were the "hypocrites" that Lena was now convinced they were. She really had come to love the Dinforths and enjoyed her time with them. Once she understood that Lena was not the nasty, unpleasant person she at first appeared to be, that is. Lena had explained that because of the severe rheumatoid arthritis that had now bowed her over and deformed her hands a bit she was almost always in pain.

She had medications, but they made her sleep a lot, and even though Moses was ten years old and big enough to do most things for himself, she knew he needed her to be as attentive to him as she could possibly be.

He had already been held back in the second-grade due to missing so many days. That was back when she was taking the medications as she had been instructed and couldn't wake up in time to get Moses up and out the door.

Lena said she would never forgive herself for that and vowed she would never do that to him again. "My grandson is an intelligent, polite young man and he deserves the best I can give him. That may not be much, but I just know one day that boy is going to have the wonderful life he deserves. And I'm determined to at least start him on that path." BINGO, Rita thought.

Lena wanted Moses to have the best she could give him, and the best she could give him was Jesus. As Lena continued to talk, Rita silently prayed, "Lord, help Lena to see and understand that introducing Moses to Your Son, Jesus, IS the best she can give him." "… to help out, even some mornings before he goes to school."

Rita hated to admit that she had missed part of that sentence and asked Lena what she'd said. Lena chuckled, "Rita, are you getting hard of hearing?"

They both laughed, then Lena repeated herself. "I was telling you that Moses does little odd jobs to earn a little money. Bless his heart, he wants to help out around here. I thank him for wanting to help, but I always tell him that he earns the money, it's his. I do encourage him to spend a little and save a little though."

"A lot of times he will set some of the neighbor's garbage out before he goes to school. And more often than not, he'll get his clothes dirty. I hate for him to go to school like that, don't want people to think he doesn't have clean clothes. They may not be the nice, fancy, expensive clothes most of the other kids wear, but I do my best to make sure they're clean."

"He already gets picked on because he stutters and because he's different from the other boys. Moses is a polite, caring boy and gets made fun of a lot for just being who he is. So you know wearing dirty and sometimes smelly clothes to school from putting out the garbage only makes it worse. At one time, I made him stop doing it, but the poor child seemed so sad about it. I didn't have the heart to stick to it."

"I guess making his own little money makes him feel good about himself somehow. I've asked the neighbors to let him put the garbage out at night, and a few tried that, but loose dogs knocked the cans over and strewed garbage everywhere."

"On school days Moses just doesn't have time to pick all that up, and most of his 'customers' are elderly and ailing widows like herself who aren't able to do it for themselves."

"Why it was because of the dogs that Moses put their own cans out in the morning instead of at night. Lena said Moses also raked leaves, and often ran to the store for some of the same neighbors."

"They like and trust him a lot." That last sentence Lena said with a smile so bright that Rita thought it could light up a room on a dark night. She wasn't his grandmother, but she was proud of this young man too. "Yes, Moses was indeed an exceptional boy."

Rita and the Dinforths had continued in their friendship, so she didn't miss working anymore and she didn't feel so lonely anymore either. She was happy that she had someone to be a blessing to in some small way. And she was blessed by their friendship as well. As often as she could, Rita even arranged her shopping days to coincide with days she knew Lena needed to go out. She did this because not only did she enjoy it, but she knew Lena wouldn't ordinarily call and ask her for anything, unless she absolutely had to.

It was now the middle of October and Rita had her mind on Thanksgiving and Christmas. Since becoming an employed adult, she had always been one to get her shopping done early, usually starting mid to late October.

Every year that she was a teacher, she always made sure she carried some extra special treat for the Thanksgiving and Christmas parties they had at school. Usually homemade cookies, one big cookie for each child, and some small stocking stuffer. She was usually done with Christmas shopping by the end of November. Of course, when she and her John Henry got married, she had the extra special joy of shopping for him and for the kids.

How she had loved almost agonizing over each gift, wanting to make sure each gift was just right for each one of them. And on Christmas morning, nothing could compare to the delight she saw on their faces when they opened their gifts. But she no longer had her sweet, precious John to buy for.

Last year she and her stepchildren had tried to celebrate Christmas together, but it just wasn't the same without her husband and their father. This year she would make sure that she packaged up the gifts for the kids and grandkids and send them in plenty of time for the packages to arrive before Christmas day. And she knew that Ricky and Jackie Sue would do the same for her, especially since they'd decided not to get together this year.

The kids' workloads were such that they couldn't take much time off for the holidays. And even though she knew they loved her, she also knew that the loss of their dear father was still too fresh for them. But they wanted her to know that their love for her had not changed, and wanted her to just remember that.

She again thanked God for blessing her with such wonderful stepchildren that loved her so much. And my, oh my! How she loved them. She was free to visit Ricky and his family, but she thought she would just stay home. And now that she had the Dinforths, she was glad she'd made that decision. In her heart she thought that maybe, just maybe she might see an answer to her prayers for Lena and Moses Dinforth during the holidays, God willing

Two weeks before Thanksgiving, Rita and Lena were out for grocery shopping together. Rita made sure to stay close by her friend because she could tell the cold weather was wreaking havoc on the arthritic Lena. She seemed to be stooped over a little more and she was moving even slower. Even Lena's smile seemed pained at times. She noticed all this but said nothing because she knew the last thing Lena Dinforth wanted was pity from anyone. If anything could end their friendship, that was it. Besides, it was Saturday. Moses was out of school and she knew that he wouldn't get too far away from his grandmother.

Those two really loved each other and it did Rita's heart so much good to see that, and even more so to be blessed enough to be a part of the love they shared. After the grocery shopping was done and they were about to check out, Lena noticed how many groceries were in Rita's cart, and began to laugh, a rich and hearty laugh that made other people turn to see what was so funny.

Rita and Moses both smiled and exchanged puzzled glances. "What's s-s- so funny G-Grandma?" Moses asked.

Lena's response was more laughter. She was laughing at the sight of her dear sweet, and really short friend Rita, who was 5'1", pushing a shopping cart piled so high that she could barely see over it. Lena was able to control her laughter long enough to get checked out and to wait for Rita. But after her friend was checked out, and the groceries were once again piled in the cart, she couldn't contain it any longer.

She laughed all the way to the car. People they passed along the way smiled and even laughed with puzzled expressions on their faces. They had no clue what was so funny, but Lena's laughter just seemed to invite them to join in. Rita and Moses were as much in the dark as the passersby, but that infectious laughter had gotten hold of them as well.

Once they were in the car and Lena had been able to compose herself, Moses asked again what had been so funny. Lena laughed again, but not as much this time. She said, "Rita, I never realized that you're even shorter than I am. Seeing you peeping over that cart as you pushed it was just so funny to me. I can't explain why, but Rita it was so funny to me".

Now, as Rita had a mental image of herself behind that loaded cart, she began to laugh so hard that she was crying, which started Lena back to laughing. Moses, seeing the two women, the two people who meant all the world to him laughing so hard, joined in. None of them realized that the laughter was what they all needed.

Once they were composed some few minutes later, Lena confessed to Rita that she couldn't remember the last time she had laughed like that. And to hear Moses laugh that way was priceless to them both. Suddenly, Lena said something so unexpected, that for a moment Rita and Moses were both in shock.

She said, "Rita, Moses is the only other person I say this to, but I really do love you. You're a true friend to us, and you're a true Christian. When I first met you in the Sav-a-Lot, I thought that like his last teacher you would try to convince me that Moses was a bad boy."

"According to her, he was always causing trouble. Only that the things she would accuse him of made no sense. They were out of character for him. He's not a bully. If anything he was being bullied, but she never wanted to hear that."

"But I know you have a heart for my grandson. You love that boy because you see the good in him, and I appreciate that. And I'm glad you cared enough to get to know me, which I know hasn't been easy. I love you Rita, and I just want to say thank you for being the wonderful friend that you are".

With grateful tears in her eyes, Rita told them both that she loved them too and that not a day went by that she didn't thank the good Lord for them. And those weren't empty words, she meant it.

When they got back to the Dinforth's home and had unloaded the groceries, they all sat in the living room and talked while they sipped hot chocolate. Moses had turned on the television and had become captivated by a commercial. It was for a Nintendo 3DS. She would be the first to admit that she knew nothing about such things but was determined that God willing, Moses would have one come Christmas morning.

She never let on to what she was thinking, but made a mental note to remember that particular game, or whatever it was called. After chatting a while longer, she told Lena why she had bought so many groceries. "I'm here with you and Moses so much, but we've never been together in my home. I'm really hoping that you and Moses will have Thanksgiving dinner with me."

Lena's eyes filled with tears as she asked, "Are you sure that won't be too much trouble for you?" "Nothing of that sort," replied Rita. "How about it Moses? Would you mind spending Thanksgiving with an old teacher?"

He smiled a beautifully bright smile and assured her he would love it. She had no way of knowing that since she had been coming around and was so good to both his grandmother and him, he wished with all of his ten-year-old heart that the three of them could live together. Moses was a loner. He used to try to fit in with the other kids, but it always ended up with most of them making fun of his stutter, calling him "Stinky Stutter Moses", or even with some of the boys shoving him around. That last hadn't happened since he'd gotten mad and punched Dinky Garrison in the nose.

He knew it was wrong to fight and was afraid he would get in trouble, but he just couldn't take it anymore. For days after that, Moses was on pins and needles, expecting to be called to the principal's office, but since no one told on him, he never was. And he never told his grandma about it either. And he continued getting used to being left alone.

He didn't like the names they called him, but it was getting to the point that most of the time he didn't really feel anything anymore. When he was with his grandma, and now with Miss Rita, they made him feel loved and wanted. It was at school that he didn't feel very good about himself because he wasn't like the other boys and the way they treated him, and because of his stutter.

At ten years old, he couldn't understand his thoughts well enough to articulate them. All he knew was that these ladies made him feel special. He knew they loved him and always wanted him around. So, yes, he would love spending Thanksgiving with these two women.

Thanksgiving Day came and went. Rita and the Dinforths had laughed and eaten, and eaten and laughed. When it was time to carry them back home, Rita packed a big box of food to take home with them. She said there was no way she would ever eat that much food, and with young Moses being a growing boy, she knew it wouldn't go to waste. They all laughed.

The truth was, Rita had deliberately overcooked figuring that was one way Lena would let her help with food for her and Moses. Lena insisted that she and Moses help clean the kitchen, and then Rita drove them home. As they said their goodbyes, Rita felt sadness creep up in her. She didn't want the day to end. Now she had to go back home to an empty house, knowing her dearly beloved John Henry wasn't there.

Christmas day was swiftly approaching. Rita had already shipped all the gifts to the kids and grandkids and she'd done her shopping for the kids on her block, which had been her habit for years.

She had also bought and wrapped presents for Lena and Moses. For Lena, she'd bought an electric blanket that she hoped would alleviate some of her pain when the nights were chilly. She'd also bought her a Snuggy to wrap up in during the day as she watched television or read a book. And after knowing what Lena was giving Moses, clothes and a new bike, Rita had purchased him the Nintendo 3DS. She'd also purchased three games that the saleswoman had said were popular among his age group. Rita had been explicitly clear that she didn't want any exceptionally violent games. Not for her Moses.

Christmas day finally came. Rita arrived at the Dinforth home bearing gifts, and the part of the Christmas dinner she and Lena had agreed that she would prepare. Rita noticed the tree in the corner of the living room. When she'd visited a week ago, it wasn't there. She couldn't help admiring it for she could tell it had been decorated with a lot of love, much care, and patience.

And that angel on top of the tree for some reason seemed a little familiar, but she didn't know why. (She didn't remember that her Nana Ruth had put an angel just like that one on top of their Christmas tree when Rita was a very little girl). She didn't realize she had stood still for a couple of minutes until Moses asked, "Miss R-R- Rita, is something wrong?"

She hugged him and told him nothing was wrong, nothing at all. She was just admiring their beautiful tree and thinking how much they must have enjoyed putting it up.

Once they had brought in almost everything from her car, it was time to open presents. Since she always said grace over meals whenever they ate together, she hoped they would allow her to say a short prayer on this special day. Still, she was surprised when Lena, with no hesitation, responded, "I was hoping you would. Come on Moses. Bow your head and close your eyes".

And Rita prayed. "Lord, we thank You for this, another opportunity to celebrate the birth of Your dear and precious Son, Jesus Christ. Help us to remember that while we enjoy our families and friends, our dinners, and opening our presents, Your Son is the greatest gift anyone could ever receive."

"For that Lord, we say thank You. And sweet Jesus, to You we say, Happy Birthday. And Lord God Almighty, I thank You for loving me enough to bless me with the gift of having Lena and young Moses in my life. Thank You for the difference they have made. And Lord, I pray, let me make a difference in their lives as well. In Jesus name, Amen."

When she opened her eyes, she saw that Lena was crying silently. And young Moses, perhaps because he saw his grandmother crying, had tears in his eyes as well. They just sat in that blessed and companionable silence for a few minutes. Lena finally wiped her face, cleared her throat and declared it to be time to open gifts.

As with any ten- year- old on Christmas day, Moses thanked his grandma for the new clothes but wasn't overly thrilled about them. Lena and Rita exchanged glances and smiles as Lena asked Moses to look out in the garage to see if she'd left their little toolkit out there, she remembered something she needed to do. "Ok-k-kay G-G-Grandma."

A few seconds later, they knew he had found the bike his grandmother had gotten him for Christmas. He came tearing back into the house, so happy that he couldn't even stutter, much less talk. He hugged his grandmother and smothered her face with kisses. She told him he could ride it a little before they ate. She didn't have to say it twice, he was out of there.

While he was outside, the two women talked and set the table for dinner. They kept watch as Moses rode his bike up and down the block, and they even saw some of the other kids admiring it, which they could see made him very proud and happy. "I still think you should have given him your gift first, Rita. All that money you spent."

Rita still felt that it was only right that he open gifts from his grandmother first, no matter how much money was spent. After dinner, it would be about time for him to put the bike away anyway, so they could exchange the rest of the gifts then.

Just as they'd done on Thanksgiving, the three of them laughed through the whole meal. Anyone passing by would have declared there were more than three people in there. They also would have thought "that sure is a really happy family". After dinner, while Moses rode his bike just a little longer, Rita and Lena worked at cleaning the kitchen a little. They knew they would all be back for more, so no need to do too much right then.

When it started getting dark, Lena asked Rita to call Moses in. That's when Rita had an idea and told Lena her plan. She went to the door. "Moses, your grandmother says it's time to come in now." Hesitantly, he put the bike in the garage and locked it. When he started to come inside, Rita popped her trunk and asked Moses if he thought he could help her bring in some more packages. He hadn't mentioned that she had only given his grandmother presents. "After the bike, he probably didn't care", she thought as she smiled.

When they went to the car, Moses saw not one, but two big gifts with his name on them, as well as a couple of other gifts with no name on them. His eyes stretched wide open and his mouth did the same. "For me? These are for me?"

Rita assured him that those gifts were his. She let him carry the one with the gaming system and she carried the other gifts. He really wanted to run inside, but didn't. Once inside, he tore off the pretty paper and ribbon. When he saw what was inside, the Nintendo 3DS, he was speechless again.

He jumped up and hugged Rita and smothered her face with kisses just as he had done with his grandmother. She thanked God for allowing her to be a part of this precious child's happiness. He went back to the game and was getting ready to play.

That's when Rita reminded him of the second gift. "Moses, don't you want to see what's in this other package?" Lena looked at Rita with a puzzled look.

Rita just smiled and shrugged her shoulders. When he got it open not only did he appear to be in shock, but his grandmother did as well. It was a small flat screen TV. Once again, when she looked at Lena, the grandmother's eyes were filled with tears. The other packages contained jacket and sneakers for him.

When Moses had left the room to carry the TV to his own room, Lena, smiling, said, "I said it before and I'm saying it again. Rita Lesslee, I know you definitely have a heart full of love for us. But what makes me love and appreciate you even more is the love in your heart for my grandson. And I still say you spent too much money on us. Especially since we couldn't get a present for you."

Rita knew that Lena had spent what money she had to get Moses' Christmas gifts. She had also been around them long enough to know that Lena got one check per month and that once she paid bills and bought food, there wasn't very much left. She had tried her best to convince Lena to let her pay for the food for dinner, but that proud woman wouldn't hear of it. But her friend would not stop Rita from doing all she could to make this a very happy Christmas for them. She didn't care that they couldn't give her a present.

The one she got in just being their friend, in being allowed to share in their joy, especially on this Christmas day was all the present she needed, and then some, and she told her friend so.

In true Christmas dinner fashion, they all found themselves back in the kitchen, for desserts this time. There were sweet potato pie, pumpkin pie, cherry cheesecake, chocolate cake and red velvet cake. All three of them decided to take a tiny piece of everything and when they finished eating they could hardly move.

Moses went in the living room to play with his 3DS. As Lena and Rita put food away and cleaned the kitchen, Lena spoke the sweetest words to her she had heard in a long time.

"Rita, I don't know if this is much of a gift for you, but I would like Moses and I to go with you to church Sunday."

Before she knew it Rita shouted out "Hallelujah! Thank You Jesus!"

Moses, not knowing what was going on, came running back into the kitchen, where both women assured him there was nothing wrong. His grandmother told him of the gift they were going to give to Miss Rita, and Moses smiled and hugged both ladies. He was glad to see them so happy, especially his grandmother.

That Sunday morning there was a bit of snow on the ground and Rita was afraid Lena would change her mind. If that was the case, she would understand. By the grace of God, she didn't have any real ailments, but she had seen others, especially Lena suffer with them. She prayed for her friend. Just as she said "Amen" the phone rang. It was Lena. "Just because there's a little snow on the ground does not mean we're not going with you to church. We've walked to the store in much worse than this. We'll be ready and waiting."

When they arrived at the Living Word Holiness Church, Lena hesitated to open the car door. "What's wrong?" Rita asked, fearing that her friend had changed her mind. "Oh. Nothing! It's just been a long time since Moses and I have set foot in a church, too long." Rita smiled, reached across and grabbed her friend's hand and gave it a squeeze.

Once the service was over and they were headed back to the Dinforth's, Lena told Rita she knew that Word was for her. The subject had been, 'DO YOU WANT TO BE FORGIVEN" The Scripture had been Matthew 6:14-15. "For if you forgive other people when they sin against you, your heavenly Father will also forgive you. But if you do not forgive others their sins, your Father will not forgive your sins." There were other Scriptures, but that stuck foremost in Lena's mind.

The pastor went on to explain how unforgiveness eats at you like cancer. It robs you of your joy, your peace, relationships, even your health. At this point she had forgotten the pastor's name, but he definitely had her full attention. Rita's heart rejoiced at the thought of Lena receiving this word.

She'd looked at Moses and saw that like any ten-year-old child experiencing something for the first time, he had been looking all around in awe of his surroundings. Lena didn't see this, for she was captivated by the word that was coming forth. Near the end of the sermon, the pastor focused on love. She remembered 1Peter 4:8, "Above all, love each other deeply, because love covers over a multitude of sins."

His closing lines were, "So, my brothers and sisters, do you want to hold on to the unforgiveness in your heart that you know is killing you, and not be forgiven by God? Or do you want to be forgiven and live the abundant life God means for you to have? Only you can make that choice."

The rest of the drive home was filled with Moses recalling all he had seen. He didn't know much about the preaching, but he really liked the singing, and wanted to go back and hear some more of it.

When they reached the Dinforth's home, Rita declined the invitation to go in because she was expecting a phone call. When she had called Ricky the night before, he'd had to take a long distance business call, but promised to call her sometime after they were all out of church on Sunday.

As she left the Dinforths and drove to her own house, Rita could hardly contain herself, praising the Lord all the way! She was so thankful that her prayers for Lena and Moses were being answered and that God was using her for His glory! Using her as an instrument to make the difference in their lives.

On that following Monday, Lena called to tell Rita that she and Moses wanted to attend watch night service if they were going to have it. Rita assured her that they were having the service, and did herself a little praise dance when she got off the phone. "Lord, thank You for continuing to make that difference," she shouted into the atmosphere of her home.

At 10 p.m. on December 31st, watch service started. It was a mini-concert and there was a heavy and tangible Spirit of praise and worship in the atmosphere. Moses was so enthralled by the music that he sat on the edge of his seat.

When she looked over at Lena, she saw her friend lost in worship, and that was all Rita knew for quite a while, for she was lost in worship herself. She'd had a lot to be grateful for even before she met the Dinforths. But now that they were in her life, her heart was so full she thought it would burst from gratefulness.

At midnight the concert ended, but the worship didn't. The atmosphere was so heavy in the church that no one wanted to leave. Some people were kneeling at the altar. Some were lying prostrate. Some were walking around the church. Some were still seated and crying. Finally, when the Presence began to lift, Rita wiped her face and looked over at Moses, who had fallen asleep, and Lena. Only Lena wasn't there. She looked around, thinking her friend might be in the bathroom.

When she got up to go see about her, out of the corner of her eye, she caught a familiar movement at the altar. It was Lena!! She had been kneeling at the altar! As she was making her way back to her seat, Rita went to meet her. Neither of them spoke. They just held each other and cried for what could have been five minutes or an hour. All they knew was that when they started toward their seat, the church was all but empty. They woke up Moses and headed to the car, each still in the residual throes of worship.

On New Year Day, Rita did something she didn't do very often unless she was sick with flu or a virus. She stayed in bed until noon that day and felt like she could have stayed longer. She was still a little tired given that she hadn't gone to sleep until almost five that morning.

She was in bed shortly after three, but she was too excited to sleep. She couldn't stop thinking about her dear friend, Lena, getting up after kneeling at the altar. She thought about how her own life had changed since meeting Moses Dinforth on the first day of school when she substituted for one of the full time teachers. She realized that God had given her a heart for Moses (as Lena had termed it).

He had also given her a heart for her dear friend, his grandmother, Lena Dinsforth. And she definitely knew that He had given them a heart for her as well, and for that, she was truly thankful.

Later that afternoon, Rita called to check on the Dinforths and to wish them once again a very happy new year. She spoke with Moses for a bit and then she and Lena chatted for a while. Mostly about the awesome move of God at watch night service. Rita had the feeling that there was something else, something special that Lena wanted to say, but didn't. She wondered what it might be.

Later that week when they went shopping together, she hoped her friend would tell her whatever that thing might be, but she didn't. She began to think that maybe she was wrong. Then on the following Saturday Lena had called to ask Rita if she could come over. It wasn't an emergency, but it was important.

In less than an hour, Rita was walking into the Dinforth's house, worried that something was wrong. As soon as they all spoke to one another, she asked Lena what was wrong. Before Lena answered her, she said, "Sit down please Rita. Would you like something to drink?" "No, thank you." Rita was wondering why Lena was being so formal. What could she have said or done to upset her dear friend? Whatever it was, Rita just wanted to make it right. She said a short prayer. She didn't know that Lena could hardly keep herself from blurting out what she wanted to tell Rita.

Finally, Lena sat down and turned to Rita. She Said, "Rita, I have some things to say to you and I must ask you to please just listen. Will you do that?" Rita promised she would.

Her friend began to talk. "Rita, when I first met you, I assumed that you were like so many other people, looking down your nose at Moses and me. When you offered us a ride home from the Sav-a-Lot, I didn't trust you."

"But when you sat here and talked with me that day, I knew you were different. You didn't talk AT me or down to me. You talked TO me."

"And what surprised me even more was that you listened to me! I mean you really listened instead of pretending to."

"When you left here that day, I had a feeling that you were a child of God, but I had to be sure. So many people claim to be what they're not these days. As time has passed, I have watched you and you have never changed. You have always been loving, kind and helpful."

"But you really won my respect even more by not trying to force me to come to church with you. You offered, I refused, and you respected that. But I also knew that you didn't leave it alone though."

For a while now, I have had the feeling that you have been praying for my grandson and me. I know I'm taking the long way around to say that Moses and I love you Rita. And you always show that you love us in so many ways. I'm so glad you didn't give up on us."

"And I'm even gladder that you didn't stop praying for us. You're a real friend and a true Christian Rita. And I thank God for you."

"Now, to get to the main thing I want to tell you. On Tuesday, I called your Pastor Lark. I told him about you and the difference God used you to make in our lives. Rita, since God brought you into our lives, I have had to really look at myself, at my life."

"I had to face the fact that all these years I have let unforgiveness rule my heart and my life, and by default, it's ruled Moses' young life. I love that boy with all my heart, and yet, I've been cheating him out of the main thing he needs. I should have been teaching him about the love of Jesus. I should have had him in Sunday school. I should have been teaching him to pray over his food, and to thank God for our blessings."

"I should have been teaching him so many things that I had learned about our Savior, Jesus Christ. But because of my own selfishness and unforgiveness, I didn't."

"God knows I am so sorry for all the wrong I've done, and I have asked God to forgive me and cleanse me through and through. And now, tomorrow morning, Pastor Lark has agreed to baptize me!"

"That's right Rita! I'm committing my way unto the Lord! Not only has God joined our hearts in friendship, but He has also made us sisters in Him! And just think, all this happened because He gave you a heart for Moses!"

SCRIPTURES:

Psalm 139:14….. I will praise thee; for I am fearfully and wonderfully made: marvelous are thy works; and that my soul knoweth right well. (KJV)

Matthew 6:14-15….. For if you forgive other people when they sin against you, your heavenly Father will also forgive you. But if you do not forgive others their sins, your Father will not forgive your sins. (NIV)

www.ingramcontent.com/pod-product-compliance
Lightning Source LLC
LaVergne TN
LVHW041537060526
838200LV00037B/1025